Summer in February

A memoir of Lima, Peru and its beaches

Marie Alvarez-Calderon

Quality Insights, LLC

Author: Alvarez-Calderon, Marie
Summer in February: a memoir of Lima, Peru and its beaches

This book is a work of nonfiction, created from the author's notes and memory. For privacy reasons, the names of some persons and locations have been changed.

Published by Quality Insights, LLC, January 2010
First printing in United States by Lightning Source, LLC

LIBRARY OF CONGRESS CATALOGING-IN-PUBLICATION DATA
ISBN 978-0-9843929-0-2 (paperback)
ISTC A03-2009-0000000A-2

Cover photo and layout by Jaime Alvarez-Calderon

Categories:
1. Life Stories
2. Women-Peru-Lima-Social life and customs
3. Peruvian travel
4. Beach life
5. Religious art
6. Domestic violence-spouse abuse

"Then a great and powerful wind tore the mountains apart ...
After the wind there was an earthquake...
After the earthquake came a fire...
And after the fire came a gentle whisper. "
I Kings 19:11-12

And it said to me, *"Let go."*

To Jaime

Contigo aprendí...
Que yo nací el día que te conocí.

With you I have understood ...
That I was born the day I met you.

Peru is a democratic nation of over 28 million people. The size of California, Texas, and Florida combined; its archeological ruins date back almost 5,000 years.

Located on the Pacific side of South America, Peru's terrain consists of three vertical bands: the desert coast, the mighty Andes and the jungle, from which flow the headwaters of the Amazon River.

Birthplace of pima cotton, potatoes, amaranth, quinoa and sweet potatoes, Peru produces a wealth of other agricultural products. It is rich in natural resources, such as gold, silver, copper, and natural gas.

A third of the country's population lives in Lima, a city founded by Francisco Pizarro in 1535. Today this cosmopolitan capital is home to 9,000,000 people.

As one of the few capitals in the world located directly on the ocean, Lima has easy access to scores of beautiful beaches, both to the north and south.

Contents

As a freshman at Sam Houston State with a recently-knitted mohair sweater thrown casually over my shoulder, I had no idea the dangerous and exciting adventures that lay ahead.

Prologue
A Gypsy's Prophecy
1966 – 1986

The fortune teller held my left hand in hers, studying my palm. "You will not marry this one."

Of that, I was not afraid.

It was my first date with a lanky and genial college junior, who was a leader at our campus Bible Chair. He was from Groesbeck, Texas and drove an old four-door dark blue Chevy with worn seats. He'd come to pick me up one cold and dark November night. Asking where I'd like to go, he was shocked when I asked him to take me deep into the piney woods outside Huntsville, Texas – to see a fortune teller. I knew it was an outrageous request. No one else could know. We were both avowed Christian fundamentalists.

"This one, he will not hurt you," the gypsy continued.

Why would anyone hurt me? I thought.

Hidden behind a thick black curtain, with my stunned date well out of sight, she continued studying my palm. "I see a dark man."

"My future husband?"

She did not answer.

"Have I met him yet?"

"Not yet."

"How exciting! We *will* be happy, won't we?" I said hopefully.

She took a deep breath and looked past me, into the darkened room. "I see a room filled with beautiful things from all over the world," she continued.

"But *will* I have a happy marriage?" I pleaded.

"I will only say that you will have a *very* interesting life." And with that she closed my palm and began to stand up.

"I want to have four children," I said, grasping for more information. She sat back down. "Make a fist." I complied. "I see only one child."

"Oh no, that can't be. I'm a Home Economics major. My family will be *everything* to me. I want to have at least four children."

"The creases don't lie; you will only bear one child." I was devastated. "But look! What have we here?" She turned my hand over. "There may be other children. Tighten your fist so I can see them better. Yes, there will be perhaps three other children, but they will not be yours.

"That's it. Your thirty minutes are up." The gypsy stood up, threw open the heavy curtain, and motioned me outside. I pulled a wrinkled $10 bill from my coat pocket and handed it to her. It was one-fourth of my monthly allowance. We were escorted quickly outside. The front door slammed closed, leaving my date and me standing in the pitch dark. I remember walking towards the old Chevy on a carpet of aromatic pine needles. We drove without speaking down the thin unpaved and rutted road that led through the deep Texas woods and back to the campus of Sam Houston State University. I would not see him or the fortune teller again.

This man and this college did not hold the keys to my destiny. By then I had already met all the single men at our college Bible Chair. And yet I had no option to marry outside "The Church." The next semester I transferred to Abilene Christian College, where there was a larger selection of "Christian" men to choose from.

My mother tried for years to warn me, but I didn't understand what she was talking about. "I don't care who you marry," she had said. "It can be anyone – an Italian, Jew, even a Negro."

Really? I thought. After all, this was Texas in the 1960s. Schools were only integrated during my senior year in high school.

"But whatever you do, *never* marry a Latin man!" This was a strange admonition, since I didn't personally know any Italians, Jews, blacks, or Latins. The only Latin man I knew of was Ricky Ricardo on "I Love Lucy" and I preferred him over her. But mother had a lot of experience in Latin men.

Born in New York City to white Cuban immigrant parents, she went to a magnet high school and became a theatrical dress designer on Broadway. During WWII she learned to fly airplanes, and then trained to be an aircraft instrument technician. She joined the Waves and was assigned to a base on the island of Oahu, Hawaii. After the war ended, it was there that she met and married my father, a tall, fair-haired, blue-eyed engineer from Hearne, Texas.

I was born in 1948 in the mountains of Oahu outside an army base in a town called Wahiawa, which means "the place of rains." My birth was followed by an earthquake, which the locals said meant that I would become a "change maker." Before my second birthday, we moved to College Station, Texas so my father could finish his masters' degrees in Industrial and Chemical Engineering.

Growing up in Texas, I looked much like many other fair-haired, white-skinned, green-eyed girls of my generation. In those days, everyone in the southern U.S. states was keenly aware of the separation between blacks and whites – something my family deplored. But being born into a multi-cultural family, I was completely unaware that there were people so untraveled, and so culturally illiterate that they held grudges against *anyone* outside their own narrow circle. This included people with white skin and people from different countries – or even different states. If my mother faced discrimination in Texas as a Latin and a Yankee, she kept it a secret from us. But when Mother made that statement about the Italians, Jews, and Negros, she must have been assuring me that she had none of the bigotry she sensed as a Texas outsider. Still, there was her warning about Latin men. Perhaps she had been exposed to another type of Latin man, the stereotypical hot blooded, controlling, and domineering kind some people imagine.

Mother taught us that our most important assets came from being ethnically diverse. She believed that, compared to Anglos, Latins and many other ethnic groups had more joy, more style, and closer families. They traveled more, spoke more languages, cooked more creative foods using more spices, were more generous, more flexible and open-minded, had less grey hairs, less cellulite, sexier bodies, and got better tans. Of that we were sure – mother and her international friends were living proof.

In those days "National Geographic" was a hot commodity. I remember guys on our school bus passing around the latest copy, ogling photos of African women's breasts. I too had a "National Geographic" fantasy: I wanted to travel to Peru and meet its people. Being an accomplished seamstress with an acute interest in the 'feel' of textiles, I was also fascinated with Peru's unique fibers – the silky baby alpaca and cloud-like Pima cotton, both of which originated thousands of years before in that very country. Neither cloth nor clothing made from those fibers would be sold in our part of the U.S. for decades. It would be decades more before I would learn about, and finally touch, the most expensive and exotic fiber from the most illusive animal of all: vicuña.

In college I sought for ways to get to Peru. In those days, no woman I knew traveled abroad alone. Instead, adventuresome fundamentalist women married missionaries. The problem was that all the missionary students were already taken.

At Abilene Christian College my suitemate and close friend introduced me to her handsome brother, Luke, who had just been accepted to medical school in Guadalajara, Mexico. It was as close to marrying a medical missionary as I could get. Luke's father was a doctor who intended that his eldest son inherit his thriving medical practice.

My "dark man" had white skin like me, but his hair was so dark it looked black. He had beady black eyes, a hooded brow, and ears that lay flat against his head. He was descended from "black Irish" stock on his mother's side, while his father's side claimed to be direct descendents of a notorious European king. Genealogy books documented that this king had given my father's family their coat of arms. Surely, I thought, this was my destiny.

Luke was brilliant and handsome – a male model on occasion, his sister confided. He pulled up to my dorm in a deep green Oldsmobile Cutlass convertible with a white canvas top and white leather interior. In those days there was nothing like him in small-town Texas. Luke was from Dallas. I was snowed. As he escorted me out of the dorm, I noticed he was limping.

"I've made some mistakes in my past," he confessed. "But after John and I stole that plane and crashed it, and after he died, I had five months in a body cast to think about my future. God spoke to me and I listened. My college grade point average will keep me out of U.S. medical schools, but I've been accepted to the Universidad Autónoma in Guadalajara. It's a private school. After a couple of years, if I do well on the ECFMG exam, I can transfer back to the U.S. How does life in Mexico sound?"

I believed that God had spoken, that Luke had reformed, and that life with him would be a great adventure.

But when my grandmother met Luke, she wasn't impressed. "You know what he wants?" she queried me. "More."

I wondered what she meant by that. I began to doubt our relationship when that same day Luke told me, "You know you're pretty lucky to have a guy like me."

"I beg your pardon?" I sharply responded. But time has erased his answer.

Three months later, on a lovely spring afternoon, parked on the shores of White Rock Lake in Dallas, Luke lowered the top on his convertible, put his arm around me and asked if I would marry him. His family bought me a lovely three-quarter carat diamond engagement ring which caused such a stir back in the Abilene dorm that I had to sleep with my left hand facing the door so visitors could parade in and out during the night to see it. I had never planned to marry before graduating, but in those days a girl getting her "Mrs. Degree" was worth more than a MBA is today.

Luke and I were married in June 1967 in a ceremony that was preceded by weeks of torrential rain. On our wedding day my horoscope read, "A good start may be half the battle, but that's as far as some people ever get." I cut out that horoscope and taped it to the front page of our wedding book. Rushing to the ceremony, my suitemate and I virtually flew over a railroad track. My avocado green Samsonite makeup case bounced, shattering the large mirror glued to its lid. "Seven years of bad luck," she laughed prophetically. I felt a creeping chill coming up my legs.

The church was undergoing a major renovation and was completely torn apart. Over the groom's entrance was a sign with "Emergency Exit" printed in bright red letters. My father walked me down a concrete isle covered in white sheets. We never found the flowers, which were left on the front pew. The preacher got Luke's name wrong, but managed to marry us all the same. As we left the reception, well-wishers pushed rice into a large hole in the passenger side window of his convertible.

"What happened to your windshield?" I asked, stuffing the train of my wedding dress into the car and brushing off the rice.

"Oh, someone threw a beer bottle at us as we left the bachelor party," Luke quickly explained. This was all too much. I wanted to run away, but by then I knew it was too late.

We took a quick scuba diving trip to the Florida Keys, but Luke forgot his driver's license and I was too young to rent a car. Fortunately, Mother's Cuban friends in Miami saved the day by renting a car for us.

Two weeks after the wedding, we packed the Olds and headed for Guadalajara, where the first phase of my destiny awaited. An inexperienced driver, I fell asleep at the wheel and ran off the road in the Saltillo desert. Our relief at not being physically hurt was quickly overcome by the condition of the convertible and by a busload of "friendly helpers," who attempted to steal all our possessions. We were towed into a small town by a professed mechanic who, once he got us inside his house and, while his wife was feeding us chicken soup, attempted to swap our new car's battery and tires for damaged ones. All bad omens for a new marriage.

Years later I would find out that our precipitous marriage was encouraged by Luke's father, who wanted to protect his son from physical relations with those "damned Beaners." Returning from Guadalajara to visit in their Dallas home, I noticed a pump shotgun behind the master bedroom door. On a later trip, bars appeared on the windows and doors of their rambling home in a fine Dallas neighborhood, "To keep out those damn niggers," my father-in-law explained. The family treated his racial prejudice with levity, never taking him seriously. Since I'd not been exposed to anyone of his temperament, I didn't know what to think.

My father-in-law had a medical office between his bedroom and the carport. "For after-hours patients," he explained. That office contained a small safe, from which the contents often mysteriously disappeared. That was where he kept several cases of narcotics ampoules.

Occasionally, while visiting my in-laws I would hear yelling and banging behind the closed master bedroom door. Then the side door to the carport would slam, a car would start up, and my mother-in-law would drive off in her Cadillac to some small, unidentified hotel in east Texas. "She just needs a rest," the family would say. I thought this was strange, but never picked up on the clues. One tragedy followed another. I clearly remember the afternoon I called Dallas to find that Luke's brother was in a coma. He never woke up. "Accidental drug overdose," was the coroner's conclusion. Many years later his older sister would be found in her home, slumped over in a chair, dead.

In those days I didn't understand how my father-in-law's bigotry, access to narcotics, and volatile temper had sowed the seeds that would turn my handsome, brilliant young husband into the "dark man" that the fortune teller had seen in my palm. Raised by a vibrant, innovative, and loving Latin mother and a highly-disciplined and well-read engineer father, I had been carefully shielded from bigotry, drug abuse, and the domestic violence I had unwittingly married into.

The years in Mexico were filled with extremes. There were many sunny days in the dark green Olds convertible with the white leather interior. Living on $125 a month, jointly donated by both sets of parents, we somehow occasionally scraped together enough money to scuba dive in remote areas near the Pacific coastal town of Manzanillo. On one particularly beautiful day, we found ourselves north of town, diving off a beach filled with smooth black rocks. As we discussed the possibility of living permanently in Mexico, we looked up and to the right. There we admired a white flat-roofed house composed of blocky layers, set on a rocky hill overlooking the Pacific.

"I'd sure like to have a house like that some day," Luke said wistfully.

"I'd sure like to help the poor and the sick. Why don't we do both?" I proposed.

With the Viet Nam war raging, the thought of leaving paradise and returning to practice medicine in the U.S. was becoming far less enticing. We seriously entertained thoughts of never going back. Mexico had become our home.

As the years went by, my brilliant and handsome husband became reckless and dangerous. Once he and his friends purchased a truckload of shrink-wrapped marijuana bricks, stamped with a prominent red rooster decal.

Living during the school year in Guadalajara, we returned to Texas during the summers. While I was pregnant I lived in a dorm, completing my education at Texas Woman's University.

Upon our return to Guadalajara, just before Elisa was born, Luke started shooting Talwin®, a new wonder drug advertized as a "non-addictive" synthetic morphine and sold without prescription in the local pharmacies. He soon succumbed to the habit. In the years that followed I watched Luke's occasional attempts to kick the habit, jerking violently in bed. With no income of our own, he funded his habit with hot checks. I constantly feared that the bank police would find us and beat us up. Luke went out carousing most nights, but when he was at home it was worse, as he continually harassed me. One day Luke informed me that, while out on his motorcycle, he had tested out our new mace spray on a father with his family in the car. I was beginning to fear for my own life. One night Luke broke my jaw. Other nights he would fire a pistol near the bed while I slept. I was helpless to stop him. Then he tortured our pet bird to death, warning me, "See that, bitch? You're next."

Then on Christmas night, Luke started the harassing again, but this time his temper was even more violent. I excused myself to go to the bathroom to give him time to cool off. There I packed my green Samsonite makeup bag with a few basic necessities. I called a taxi, hoping to spend the night in a local hotel. Just in case things got nasty, I called the police.

When I returned to the living room, I found that Luke had been making his plans too. He grabbed my shoulders and threw me against the cold black metal front door, shoving his loaded 45-caliber revolver into my stomach. I listened in terror as Luke described how he planned my slow, miserable death, terminated by dumping my mortally wounded, but still quivering, body in the desert, just beyond viewing range of the highway to Saltillo. As he was a doctor, I was sure he knew just how to make me suffer. Fearing this was the end, I somehow gathered enough courage to slip open the door latch behind me and carefully push the door backwards.

But there was no way for me to escape, as Luke had taken the sparkplugs out of the car. My passport and visa were inside the house and so was just about everything I owned. I had called a taxi, but it wasn't there yet. I couldn't go back into the house, so put my Samsonite makeup case on the sidewalk and sat on top of it for the excruciatingly long time it took for the taxi to arrive. I saw the police drive by, but when they saw two *gringos* in a domestic dispute, they continued on their way. I remember Luke standing just inside the front door, the 45 pointed at my back, yelling over and over again "Come back in here!" The only reason Luke didn't shoot me in the back was because a night watchman was just outside, watching the disgrace of it all. Thank goodness my mother had seen this all coming and had taken Elisa, by then almost three years old, back to Texas the previous month.

An hour later the taxi arrived and took me to the house of a Canadian couple that our preacher had introduced us to some two weeks before. They put me on a bus to Saltillo the next morning, loaning me $100. An hour after they returned home, Luke was at their door, demanding that they return his "property."

I arrived in Saltillo on a cold December 26th. My parents met me at an old Holiday Inn, bringing my sister Eileen's clothes. The next day we left for the Reynosa border crossing, where my father got me across by saying we had just been in town, not into the interior, thus eliminating the need to show papers.

Before that terrible night I had been a Home Economics graduate and a loyal and respected wife of the handsome man who everyone assumed would become a successful doctor. Now I was nothing: I had no identity papers and I was a victim of something that in those days had no name. Today we know it as domestic violence.

Broken hearted, I returned to my small Texas town and put my dreams on hold. I went to work for a local chemical company and set about raising my daughter, as a single parent. I wrote the Canadians, who by that time had returned to Edmonton, sending them $100 from my first paycheck. They responded with a thank you note. My following letter and the ones after that came back stamped, "Addressee unknown." I could only think, *Perhaps they were my angels.*

Shortly after returning to Texas, I began working with our local shelter for battered women in hopes of helping others escape the fate that had crushed my family and my dreams. One night a woman named Catrina was admitted to the shelter with her two children. They had run for their lives and left without any clothing or suitcases. Catrina was married to a U.S. citizen, but she was originally from Peru. We collected money to fly Catrina and her children back to Lima, where her family could guarantee her safety. I gave Catrina my green Samsonite makeup case, with its missing mirror. Perhaps in its new incarnation, it would bring better luck.

Despite my attempts, my busy life couldn't heal my broken heart. Night time would find me on my knees, asking God why He had denied me the dream He had placed in my heart. In all those years I heard no reply, but one night there was a palpable presence, as if someone was sitting at the foot of my bed. I did not see it, nor did it speak, but after that day I no longer felt all alone.

For the next fourteen years Elisa and I would be a pair, living in a small house that my parents had bought and rented to us. It contained only females: the two of us, pictures of women and girls, a female dog and two female cats. We even had female fish. We were quite open-minded though, allowing my father to come over to mow our lawn and fix things that were broken.

I learned from my exciting and harrowing time in Mexico that love is truly blind, until marriage wakes it up. My mother lamented that by having sheltered me from life's dangerous side, I had walked straight into a life-threatening situation without seeing it.

I vowed to never become involved with anyone who could put my life in danger, or move to any place that was unsafe. In case I should ever again need an emergency refuge, I carried with me at all times a key to the women's shelter that I'd helped build.

After returning stateside my Aunt Doe wisely advised me, "Don't remarry until you are absolutely *sure* that you would move to the ends of the earth to be with your husband."

At that time, I couldn't imagine risking it all – again.

Part I
Just Visiting

1986 – 1996

Jaime and me, beginning our new life
together in Texas – and beyond.

1

Coming Home to a Dream

It is just before sunset, high on a hill overlooking the southern Pacific. I am sitting in a bamboo easy chair with plush, off-white canvas cushions in our master bedroom, which occupies the entire second floor of the main building of our beach house. Through the glass wall I'm enjoying a 120-degree view of the ocean. Nature's colors are like an artist's pallet. A mango sun is setting into a tourmaline sea. Dozens of large brick-red bougainvillea plants cascade down the rock-faced retaining wall. Across the full expanse of ocean, clouds sweep from left to right in waves of taupe and peach. Where they part, the sky is a lake of vivid Italian blue. Jet black silhouettes of fishermen climb down the charcoal cliffs on my right to settle in for a night's work. As they light their campfires and torches for the night, I feel a tremendous sense of presence; that everything is as I had dreamed it would be, so many years ago. At this moment, I am one with the universe.

But how had I arrived here? It is a perfect time for reflection.

Back in September 1966, as I left for college, my father called me into the living room and gave me some sage advice, "Honey, if you pursue your dreams they will all come true. But what you will not believe is *how* you get there." A truer statement was never made. As it turned out, the summer of my life came not in July, as I expected, but in February.

During the fourteen years following my terrifying first marriage, I concentrated on my career and on raising my daughter. I found time to date several men, but it soon became clear that we weren't good matches. Just when the situation seemed hopeless, a quiet mechanical engineer, who I knew vaguely from work, got divorced. In a casual dress environment, he wore starched shirts with button-down collars, fine wool pants, and a tweed wool sports coat with tan suede trim. People knew he was somehow different. I remember one person in our computer department referring to him as "that guy with the funny names."

Jaime Alvarez-Calderon was a Peruvian, though those uninitiated in Latin culture would never have guessed it by his blonde hair, blue eyes, and light skin. He was from Lima, Peru's immense capital city. I found Jaime quite attractive, well-spoken, sensitive, and genteel.

In early December 1986, we accidentally sat beside each other at a Bach Christmas Cantata. Talking during intermission, we found out that we had both been invited the next week to a mutual friend's open house. We agreed that he would pick me up. The night of the event, ignoring the other guests, we talked for hours in the kitchen. The open house was followed by our first *real* date on New Year's Day, dining at the local yacht club.

It was a brilliant, sunny day. As we walked between the rows of shining white yachts, we began talking about our backgrounds. Jaime's ex-wife was from the U.S. and had left him for another man. By that time, I had been divorced for fourteen years. We both had children of similar ages, whose first names we had, coincidentally, selected to work in both Spanish and English.

I thought to myself, *Hum, if we were to marry, we'd have four children. That's the exact number that the gypsy predicted all those years ago.*

Jaime's words brought me back to the present: "If you were ever to remarry, would you change your last name?" Being a Virgo, he believed in a direct approach.

"Sure. If I liked it," I answered bluntly. By then I was a business woman and also got right to the point. I wondered why this charming man was introducing such a delicate topic so soon.

After lunch Jaime drove me to his apartment. As he unlocked the door, I was apprehensive. Remembering my mother's warnings about Latin men, I braced myself for the unknown. But what transpired was not what I thought. First Jaime went upstairs to his bedroom loft and retrieved a ten-foot scroll, which he unrolled on the living room carpet.

"Let me explain who I *am*." Jaime showed me his father's lineage back to the 1200s on one side and the 900s on the other. His father's family had lived in Peru since 1726, having emigrated from Cantabria, a province of northern Spain. His mother was from southern Germany, and her family tree dated back to the 16th Century. Jaime's parents met while his father was studying electro-mechanical engineering in Darmstadt, Germany.

At last, here is another multinational, multicultural family, I sighed.

Jaime and I spent that first afternoon looking at videos he had just received of his family in Lima, celebrating Christmas and other joyous occasions. Their beauty, warmth, and sheer numbers gave me chills. They had well-tuned voices, singing together like a practiced choir. The next day a dozen red roses arrived at my house. The neighbors thought I was having a fling. *Oh dear.*

In a follow-up conversation, Jaime asked how I liked his last name. Of course I thought it was wonderful! We then began to see each other — but just as friends. We exchanged e-mails through our company's in-house computer network, since home computers had not yet been invented. As e-mail content was strictly restricted to business matters, the messages were short and to the point. "Dinner tonight at El Toro? Pick you up at 6:30." This went on for a while, until one day I received this message: "Want to go with me to the apartment hot tub tonight?" The blood rushed to my head and my hands began shaking. Dining out was one thing, but a dip in the hot tub could never be construed as a business meeting. In shock I quickly deleted the message, lest it fall into the wrong hands. As it turned out, that hot tub led to winter evenings beside a toasty fire. This was not the type of man to conduct a casual relationship; now there would be no turning back.

I found out early on that Jaime and I ate the same foods: *empanadas* (Latin semi-circular meat pies) and *arroz con pollo* (Latin chicken and rice), but we did not always agree on the recipes. I put capers and green olives in many recipes like the Cubans did, while he put capers only in fish dishes and used black olives instead of green at other times. The Spanish I had learned in Mexico didn't quite match with his Peruvian Spanish. One day when we were making a cake, I asked what type of *betún* (icing in Mexico) we would make. He laughed, saying that in Peru, *betún* meant shoe polish! Cilantro was called *culantro*; shrimp were called *camarones* in Mexico, but *langostinos* in Peru. I was only beginning to recognize how much I had to learn to fit into a Peruvian's life.

After we had been dating for several months, my mother asked Jaime point blank, "Where is this relationship going?" I nearly fainted from embarrassment. After all, I *was* thirty-eight years old. Surely I could handle this relationship without outside intervention!

That same day, on the way back to his apartment, Jaime asked, "So when would you like to get married?" Not the type of proposal expected for a first marriage, but properly asked and accepted for a second. We began a house search that lasted for months, complete with a spreadsheet graphing available property locations versus size, schools, and cost. In early September we bought a 40-year-old house in my parents' neighborhood. It had a good floor plan and was big enough to house our future family of six, as well as our accumulated possessions. We married in a friend's house on October 17, 1987. Following a one-day honeymoon to San Antonio, we moved into our first home.

The next four months I reviewed the videos in earnest, doing my best to memorize all the names and relationships in Jaime's Peruvian family. Still I wondered, *Would the family accept me? Would I be able to communicate with them? Would I relate to them in any way? What would I wear? How would it feel to be on the other side of the equator, where water drained in the other direction and the seasons were reversed?*

My first trip to Peru was in February 1988, four months after we married; a wedding gift from Jaime's parents. Arriving in Lima, we were met by a score of the "immediate" family, who arrived in several cars. I had met my future in-laws, Paco and Hiltrud, during their June visit to Texas the year before, but I recognized the rest of the family from the videos. Jaime's oldest brother was the first one to talk his way through the airport security guards. He came running towards me with open arms, an open face, and a broad smile, "*¡Soy Jorge!*" he exclaimed, hugging and kissing me. The scent of his Brute cologne lingered on my clothing. What a wonderful welcome.

The warmth of the family made me quickly overlook the woefully unkempt airport with its chipped terrazzo floors and its street-side windows riddled with bullet holes. As we traveled away from the airport and into cool, clammy night, I noticed that the buildings were crusted with a mixture of dirt and residual soot from auto fumes. Masses of poor people were huddled around curbside fires fueled by newspapers and burning tires.

"Lock your doors," Jaime's father warned us. "This has always been a bad area, but now it is particularly dangerous." Streetlights were blown out; the esplanades and parks were bare of vegetation and adorned with three-foot high piles of refuse.

I silently thought, *Oh no, what has my 'knight in shining armor' gotten me into?*

But the scenery began to change for the better as we moved into the luxurious San Isidro district. I was overwhelmed at how similar the construction styles were to those in the best districts of Guadalajara.

Pressing my nose against the glass, in tears I cried out, "I'M BACK! I'M BACK!"

"But you've never *been* here before," Paco said.

Perhaps not, but my heart had been preparing for this moment for years.

San Isidro was filled with elegant old homes; some so large they could easily be mistaken for hotels or even small castles. Many were in disrepair. Everywhere there were tall eucalyptus and enormous palm trees. A few red and yellow cannas bloomed in the parks. Avenida Javier Prado, the "main drag," was a mix of old mansions and modern, high-rise apartments.

We drove to the adjoining district of Miraflores, where we turned down another broad street, Avenida Pardo, with its distinctive old lamp posts bearing round globes.

"This is where I grew up," Jaime said, pointing to a dull green ten-story building with a sign "*Copias*" advertising a store that made copies. But I didn't see the building at all, because Paco and Hiltrud were busy describing their house, sold and demolished decades before. In my mind's eye, I saw the elegant mansions that once lined the avenue. A census had listed their house as having sixty-four rooms. Several employees helped manage the home, including keeping an eye on Jaime and his brothers and sisters – five siblings in all. From Jaime's lively descriptions, I could imagine the children running through the grand old house. In those days Jorge would have been about 12, Lichi 10, Tere 8, Paco 6, and Jaime 4. There were stories of get-togethers with more than thirty first cousins, each with his or her own nanny. There was even Señora Julia, the grandmother's maid, who had lost her mind but stayed on as a part of the extended family, always in the kitchen.

"Wasn't it a bit strange to keep a deranged maid around?" I asked.

"But, where else would she go?" was Hiltrud's puzzled reply.

We drove west to an adjacent district, Chacarilla, and a street called Caminos del Inca, the location of the current family home. It was built in the 1960s, when the area was little more than fields. By the 1980s, a struggling grocery store, Galax, was built a block down, across the avenue. Gone were the fields and farms; present was the packed dirt, the dust, the garbage, and the traffic.

We pulled up at the front gate and honked the horn. Uniformed maids ran out to open the large wooden doors, shutting and bolting them quickly behind the car. I noticed that there was an outer wall with a high-voltage security system, its red lights blinking on and off to warn anyone who might dare to scale the wall.

"Why do you need a security system?" I innocently asked Hiltrud.

"Lima was once a beautiful city, but we have had several governments that have not done well," Hiltrud warned. "These days there are many thieves who break into homes. Going outside alone can also be dangerous. You shouldn't go outside by yourself." I took Hiltrud at her word and focused on life inside the walls. And there was a lot to focus on.

The multi-layer family home was 6,000 square feet. The floor plan was complicated, like a set of building blocks on three levels that equaled two stories. The maids' quarters were attached too, but were separated from the main house by doors and a hidden winding staircase. It took me a couple of days to grasp the extent of it all. The house had been built to accommodate an impressive collection of old Peruvian church-size religious oils and antique hand-carved doors from Cuzco.

Over a period of days, I was introduced to more of Jaime's family. Their visits began just before lunchtime and lasted until just before nightfall. In the late mornings my stomach churned for hours, as lunch was served no earlier than 1:30 p.m. But it was worth the wait. Tantalizing and exotic aromas filled the air, as food streamed out of the kitchen, all invisibly prepared behind the swinging kitchen door. While we ate, a little bell hidden under the gold-tone carpet allowed Hiltrud to summon the maids to change courses. Sumptuous dining and seemingly unending socializing were the order of the day. The electricity went out several times in the evenings, but having lived in Mexico, I was familiar with the joys of candlelight.

As long as I stayed within the walls, there was no hint of the chaos of the outside world. One day I ventured into the room-sized pantry to find a small warehouse of canned food and dry goods. I asked Hiltrud about the need for this, with the Galax and fruit stands so nearby. Then she told me of the terrible food shortages; problems created by *Sendero Luminoso*, Shining Path terrorists blockading the roads leading into Lima.

The house and its grounds were large and there were enough visitors to entertain me for several days, but eventually I wanted to go for a walk. When Jaime and I finally went outside the walls, we were greeted by a reality more stark than I had could have ever imagined.

There was no connection between life inside and outside the walls. Inside there was family, joy, warmth, service, and style. Outside there was dirt, destruction, garbage, and food shortages. There were long lines to buy everything. The shelves of the Galax were virtually bare. Inflation was so high that people were paid *daily* in dollars, which were exchanged outside stores into intis, the currency of the day. Gas shortages and lack of spare parts resulted in abandoned vehicles, especially large buses, stopped on the sides of the road, propped up on bricks, with their wheels stolen and parts of the motor scavenged. Some had been fire bombed.

The pull of this family was strong. The energy and love that was shared between them knew no boundaries. It was like having a silk cord tied around my heart that wouldn't let go. I thought to myself, *How can this family endure so many problems? What kind of life would I have with them?* Growing up in Texas, during an affluent period in history, I couldn't imagine how a country or a family could survive under these circumstances.

One night we left the house, winding our way through the chaos to a restaurant on the ocean, *Salto del Fraile* (The Priest's Jump), named after a priest who leapt to his death from those very rocks after being unable to marry the woman he loved. We went with Jaime's sister, Lichi, and her husband, Alfredo, a lawyer with a private practice who also taught maritime law at one of Lima's most prominent universities. We were finishing a wonderful dessert of *merengado de chirimoya,* a dessert made of stacked layers of the thinnest crisp meringue and sweetened whipped cream. After some small talk, the question begged to be asked, so I spoke up.

"Alfredo, how long can you *stay* here in Peru with all the terrorists, electricity problems, water and food shortages? Why don't you just *leave* and emigrate to a larger and more stable country – like the U.S.?" It seemed like such an obvious thought.

Alfredo looked down at the table and took a deep breath to compose himself; obviously measuring his words. Speaking in flawless unaccented English he said, "Everyone knows what is happening to this country. It is very hard to live here under these conditions. But leaving would mean that – in whatever other country – we would be..." He paused, shuddering visibly at the abhorrent thought. Staring me directly in the eye, he inhaled deeply again before finishing the sentence, "*anonymous.*"

I pondered Alfredo's statement, wondering what the problem with being anonymous was. Most of us in the U.S. were virtually anonymous. People from small towns went to big cities, far away from their families, to become just that. Then I bit my lip. There had to be some dimension of *this* culture that was so important that death would be preferable to losing one's identity.

Not long afterward, Alfredo died, still resolutely in Lima, of painful cancer of the pancreas brought on by the extreme stress of living in such a dangerous and unstable environment. Things would get worse – a lot worse – before they got better. Many Peruvians left the country seeking asylum in other lands, but Jaime's family stood firm. They never left their homes.

I valued this culture, but I also valued my life in the U.S. Would I be asked to change my independent style of dress and lose my freedom of movement? Would I begin to believe that there was real danger outside, that my habits and actions were not my own, but a part of a much larger whole? I learned early on that I was dealing with *very* different ways of thinking. How would I be able to survive in two such different worlds?

My values were about to change in a major way. I began to see the profound influence of a close, loving Latin family; a love that never dimmed, not in the presence of unimaginable financial losses, lack of basic life comforts, theft, terrorism, or the expanses of continents. I was now a small part of this family and I would spend my life trying to be an instrument in passing their values on to the next generations. In those days, I could not yet imagine how to integrate Jaime's family with my life in the U.S. Only time would tell.

Yet ten years later, standing on a small horseshoe beach in a gated community, I happened to glance up and to the right and saw a white, flat-roofed home designed in cubes and arranged like a child's building blocks. It was built into a rocky cliff overlooking the Pacific. It was my home – *our* home.

It was then that I realized that Dad was right. My "lost" dreams had come true, but in ways I could never have imagined.

Jaime's parents, Hiltrud and Paco, were married in
Germany on September 5, 1939. Resisting Hitler's
government, the newlyweds escaped over the Alps,
catching a ship out of France to New York. Another
ship took them through the Panama Canal and then
on to Lima. Hiltrud would never see her father or
sister again.

2

Your Money or Your Life

Preparing for my second visit to Lima, friends in Texas began passing on their sage advice. The two most frequent comments were, "Don't drink the water" and "Watch your wallet." If this was the only advice needed, fewer tourists would become sick and no one would be robbed. Enough said? Apparently not. I could never have imagined the dangers that people in Lima were facing in the late 1980s.

One day on vacation at my in-laws' home in Lima, a dozen or so of the "intimate" family were sitting in the living room drinking our after-lunch tea, when a frightening discussion began. In case my defense mechanisms had not been sufficiently stimulated by the contrast between the life inside and outside the walls, the discussion drifted towards the many creative ways a person could be robbed. It started benignly enough.

"We went to a restaurant yesterday where a woman was screaming that her purse had been snatched," the discussion began.

"Was it hanging on her chair?"

"No."

"Was it someone who came by trying to sell papers and holding them over the plate and slipping the purse off the table?"

"No."

"Then she must have had the purse wedged behind her against the back of her chair and leaned forward."

"You guessed it."

"You can sure lose your purse fast, especially if you have a nice one. My son-in-law bought my daughter a Channel bag on his last trip to the U.S. She didn't have it a week before it was snatched."

"Yes, Lima is really becoming dangerous nowadays."

Jaime had a logical comeback, "If you look at it objectively, you have to keep your guard up anywhere you go. It's not the *place* that is dangerous, but the *thief*. I remember when a man robbed Dad of his billfold in Bad Koenig, Germany. He had just arrived the night before to visit Tío George and decided to take a walk. All his vacation money was in it!"

"If you have anything of value, think of the rule, 'If they can see it, they can steal it'," we were reminded.

Jaime tried to turn the conversation around, "I believe that the best response to any unsolicited conversation is always a quick 'No.' Grab your purse and walk quickly towards the nearest security guard or into a store – NOT back to your car."

"Maybe it's better to take a cab."

"But you have to be careful which cab you take. The easiest place to get robbed is when you leave the airport unescorted. Always hire official transportation from *inside* the airport. Step outside and you are *bait*. Never mind the official-looking uniforms or name tags; this is the perfect location for scam artists. Use any of them and you risk your pocketbook and maybe your life."

"The better looking and more expensive the taxi, the more secure it should be. Contact a reputable cab company and arrange for a drop-off and a pickup. At all costs, avoid beat-up cabs that have temporary 'Taxi' signs on the dash, especially if you are heading into a dangerous area and most especially if it is getting dark."

All this talk about theft was making me nervous. I tried to change the subject, "Nuts, anyone?"

The subject changed, but for the worse. It shifted from robbery to kidnappings, which according to the discussion, were on the rise. Kidnappers were generally classified into two categories: experienced and novice.

"All kidnappers are dangerous," I was advised. "Experienced kidnappers will rarely hurt you, knowing that they can ransom you for more money alive and in good shape. The worst type of kidnapper is one who is a novice. They kidnap you, and then they try to sell you to kidnappers who are more experienced in negotiating ransom deals. Due to their lack of experience, this process doesn't always go smoothly, and you can be maimed or even killed."

Great, I thought. *Now it seems that losing my purse is the least of my worries. Thank goodness I am a nobody here.* To date, I had not heard of any kidnappings of U.S. citizens in Lima.

The sun was getting low in the sky over the back patio wall. Guests prepared to leave.

Jaime's sister Lichi explained in her smooth, velvet-toned voice, "You know there is a *toque de queda,* a curfew strictly enforced by the police. Driving around the streets of Lima at night could get a person killed. When our teenagers go off to a party, we are terrified until they call to tell us they have arrived."

As we opened the door on the outside wall to escort our guests to their cars, Jaime's father pointed to a spot on the front driveway, "It was *right here* that the kidnappers attacked your sister Teresa."

"What?" Jaime exclaimed in horror.

This talk about kidnappings has just hit home, I thought, but was afraid to make a sound.

Jaime's father began the story, "It was on a Saturday afternoon and we had a lot of company. Tere got here late and there was no room for her to park in the carport, so she parked her car outside the walls. She knew that parking on the street wasn't safe, but she had no choice."

Tere's husband was a well-known lawyer, author, and a member of the Peruvian Senate. Time and again when the police arrested kidnappers and got hold of their "wish lists" of potential captives, his name was in the top five. This meant that his family members were also potential targets. As a senator, he received round-the-clock protection from the Peruvian equivalent of the Secret Service, but his family did not. Being some of the very few naturally light-skinned, blonde-haired, blue-eyed Peruvians, they were easily identified by people bent on doing them harm. Tere, always daring and strong, prepared to protect her family by becoming a black belt in karate and learning to shoot a gun. These were drastic measures for a Peruvian woman, where civilian ownership of weapons was practically unheard of and carrying a weapon had always been out of the question.

Jaime's father Paco continued his story, "When it was time to leave, we were escorting Tere and two of her children to their car. What we couldn't see from inside the walls was a car with several kidnappers, lying in wait at the curb. The second we unlocked the outside door, they forced their way in, grabbed Tere by the waist, and dragged her toward their car."

"Yes," Hiltrud smiled, "but they underestimated how strong Tere was."

Jaime quickly added, "When we were kids, Tere used to beat up the boys! We were all scared of her."

Hiltrud continued the story, waving her hands for emphasis, "Tere used her hands and feet to grab hold of the car's door frame, hanging on for dear life. She looked like a spider attached firmly to its web. Your father ran into the house to get something to beat the kidnappers off of her. All he could find was a broom handle, but he beat on the kidnappers with all his might."

Ana Teresa, Jaime's youngest brother's wife, broke in, "You should have seen your mother! She was the first to attack. She jumped on the man trying to force Tere into the car, like a mother bear defending her cub. But another kidnapper ran out of the car and began beating her with a night stick. He put a big gash in her head." Then, in case we needed more assurance, she added, "There was blood all over the place. Things were getting very bad, very fast. It looked like we were not going to live through this." She took a deep breath. "But Lichi saved the day!"

"How did she do that?" I couldn't imagine how anyone could live through that situation.

"Lichi didn't fight; she used her brain. She looked down the street and saw a police car coming. No one had had time to call the police – the officers coming our way must have been heading for another problem. Taking advantage of the situation, Lichi looked back at the kidnappers, screamed and pointed, 'Look, the police have come to get you!' Unnerved, the kidnappers let go of Tere, slammed their car doors, and fled."

Hiltrud shook her head, and then gently patted the back of her lovely grey hair, as if to feel the scar. Some of the family believes that the blow she took defending her daughter's life precipitated the illness which would eventually take her own.

Once safely back in the house, with the doors bolted shut, "*Flaca,* or "Skinny" as Ana Teresa was affectionately called, picked up the conversation, "You cannot *imagine* how crazy things are here. One moment we're driving down the highway, the next we're in danger of losing our lives. Did anyone tell you about when I hit that little boy?"

This was all news to me.

"A few months ago I was driving down the *Panamericana,* heading to a bridge tournament at Club Villa on the beach south of Lima. If you drive down the highway these days, you will see people all around the ditches, bathing, washing and drawing drinking water," she elaborated, her brown eyes opening wide and shaking her thick mid-length brown hair.

"Ditch water is *so* contaminated. It spreads disease, but what choice do these people have? Any water can be contaminated these days. Even Tío Guillermo (head of the esteemed Clínica Anglo-Americana) caught a bad case of cholera. He thinks he may have gotten it at his club, of all places."

I interrupted, "Cholera outbreaks! That sounds medieval. Is this a big problem?"

"It's killed 18,000 people they know about, but there are surely more."

I was getting dizzy.

Ana Teresa didn't want to lose her story, so she continued, "I was busy dodging a car coming at me from the left when, out of nowhere, this little boy ran across the busy highway. I hit him with my fender."

"And she stopped to help out," Hiltrud added, proudly.

"That's the law isn't it?" I quickly asked.

"Yes, but in these terrible times, stopping along the road in the wrong area can cost you your life," said Paco. "People can come out of the ditches and mob you."

Impatient with the interruptions, Ana Teresa concluded, "I was scared to death, for the little boy, but also for my own safety. But I had to stop. There he was, his little leg crushed by my fender. I picked him up and we took him to the hospital. His family was so grateful. They said they couldn't believe anyone would risk their own safety to stop and help."

I excused myself to go to the bathroom. All of this talk made my digestive system work overtime. Returning, the conversation focused on the kidnapping of another family member.

Ana Teresa's English was the most fluent, so she continued the conversation, "Did we tell you that my Paco was kidnapped?"

Nauseated, I wanted to run again, but stayed put on the sofa, "No, I hadn't heard that one." Jaime sat in a side chair, head down, and silent.

"Well, you know Paco is a manager for Lima's International Telephone and Telegraph. Kidnappers love to catch established businessmen, because they can extract a lot of ransom money from the company. Paco had been warned about this danger by one of the other managers," she began. "But just a few weeks afterward he was driving to a meeting in a restaurant in his business suit. At a stop light, some men jumped out from nowhere, managed to open his car door, and stabbed him in the leg. They got into his car and forced him to drive to a remote beach south of town. When they arrived at the beach, they pushed him out of the car and made him take off his slacks. Those kidnappers tried to steal his car, but found out that none of them could *drive*. Imagine! It took them a while, but in the end they drove off erratically, leaving Paco stranded there without his trousers, with his hand trying to stop his leg from bleeding!"

I didn't bother to ask how Paco got home. I couldn't take any more of these stories. They left me shaking all over. How could I ever relax while on "vacation" in Peru? After that day, it took a long time to rebuild my courage enough to venture out on the streets of even the best parts of Lima. I managed to adapt, but it was over a decade before I went out alone.

Fortunately, the situation in Peru did improve. The turnaround began in mid-1990 with the election of an entirely unpredictable presidential candidate. He was unknown to the European-descended lawyers that had previously governed the country. Alberto Fujimori, an agricultural engineer and president of the Agrarian University of Peru, was what they call a "dark horse." He parents were Japanese immigrants and totally outside the country's political circles. During his first and second terms, Peru made a major about-face. But that day in the living room, the future was far beyond the horizon.

I had a lot to learn about surviving in Lima. Growing up in Texas, with our big fenced-in yards, I never worried much about theft, and even less about kidnapping. There I trusted the police to take care of the criminals. However, I may have been the exception. I still know any number of Texans who don't feel safe unless they have guns around for protection. But the idea of being armed doesn't "fly" in many countries, where people who have guns are considered insecure, dangerous, and very often lawbreakers. Peruvians instead focus on prevention: keeping things that other people might want out of the public eye, surrounding their homes with high walls so that they are inaccessible, and if they are wise, locking their car doors *before* leaving the safety of their garages.

I have learned that we are almost always on the lookout for the obvious. The real problem is with people who sneak up on us, in a variety of ways, when our guard is down. And that is true anywhere in the world.

On the positive side, thanks to these warnings, I no longer take safety for granted. I have learned to live more in the moment; I am more *aware* of things going on around me. Valuing my safety, I am more present and more grounded, especially when in unfamiliar terrain.

Jaime and brother Paco at the Avenida Pardo house in Miraflores, Lima, c. 1956.

On board the Nusta, a yacht named after an Inca princess, near San Lorenzo Island, off the coast of Callao, c. 1955.

3

Worlds Apart

One day back in our Texas home, Jaime and I had a rare moment alone. During an otherwise quiet lunch, Jaime and I got into – not technically an argument, as Jaime was too good at interactions – but let's say we had quite a lively conversation.

I looked out the window, over our three-quarter acre green lawn, past large oak and pecan trees, and down toward the little creek that ran behind our house. It was a beautiful spring day; a good one to bring up some of the issues I was trying to deal with.

"I don't understand Peru," I began. "How can your family *stand* to live inside those walls? You've lived in Texas for years. Don't you like the big, open yards? Freedom – that's what it's all about. In the U.S. we value freedom, *personal* freedom. Yep, Life, Liberty, and the Pursuit of Happiness. It's in *our* Constitution. I didn't feel a lot of *freedom* in Lima."

"Sadly, it's true that freedom of movement isn't the same as when I grew up," replied Jaime. "When I was a young boy, I could go anywhere with my friends. I remember flying a kite on top of an Inca ruin, several blocks from our house. Now things are different, thanks to the thieves, kidnappers, terrorists, and the economic situation.

"What I like to think is that Peru is a country where we value *family harmony* even more than *personal freedom*. Peru has been subject to many types of governments, but in good times and bad, our *lifestyles* give us the freedom to be near our *families* so we can preserve our *traditions* and our *culture*. Not that we haven't suffered a lot under some of these governments. There were tough times when my father's family had to live outside the country for a while because of the political or economic climate. My dad and some of his sisters were born in Salta, Argentina, when my grandparents moved there for several years."

Jaime continued, "Speaking of *personal freedom*, it seems to me that to get ahead in the U.S., you must become a *slave* to your job. People move away from their families, to cities they don't know, work more hours, to make more money, to buy more things, many of which they *don't need*. Where does that get them?"

"Ahead." I added smugly.

"Ahead of what? In Peru, people think everyone in the U.S. spends all their time *working* instead of *enjoying their lives*. Hasn't anyone thought about the *value* of being *happy*?"

"The U.S. isn't a perfect country, but it's got the best system in the *whole world!*" I sat up a little straighter just at the thought of it.

"In what way?" Jaime queried.

"Well, *everyone* in the world wants to live in the U.S.!"

"Oh, they *do*? I wasn't aware of that. We all know that the U.S. has many wonderful things. It has the best shopping and some of the best entertainment in the world. My sisters go to New York to shop and see plays and operas. All this is wonderful, but they come back to Lima to *live.*"

"Well, you came to Texas to study engineering," I reminded him.

"That was because Eddie Marcus – you know, of Neiman-Marcus – and his wife were visiting with my uncle on our 25-foot Chris Craft one day off San Lorenzo Island near Lima. I told him I was applying for scholarships in the U.S. Then he suggested I apply for a Texas Partners scholarship."

"What did Eddie Marcus have to do with scholarships?" I didn't believe him.

"He was on the board of that program. Each state university was assigned a country. Peru was assigned to the Texas Partners program, so his connection was with the University of Texas. In fact, there are a lot of Peru connections with famous people in the U.S. John Wayne married a Peruvian."

I didn't know that, but I had a quick comeback. "So you went to study in Texas just because you talked to a rich guy on a *boat*?"

"That wasn't all. I wanted to get a technical education abroad, like my father did in Germany. The U.S. and Europe are widely recognized for their technical universities. I had already thought about getting a degree in the U.S. His suggestion just helped push me in that direction. The scholarship wasn't the only reason I came to the U.S., since it only paid a small part of my expenses."

"I'll bet you intended to *stay* in the U.S. all along," I attacked. "You just used your *scholarship* as a way to get a foot in the door. After all everyone *knows* that in the U.S. we have such an *easy* life," I said proudly.

"I am very thankful for the Mechanical Engineering degree I received at the University of Texas. But living *permanently* in the U.S. was not my original intent. I have always been proud to be a Peruvian. You and I are fortunate to have great jobs here in the U.S., but if we have such an easy life, why do we both work all day, then come home to cook our own food, do our own yard work and house repairs, wash our own clothes, and clean our own house? As two professionals, we'd *never* have to do all that in Peru." He concluded, "The U.S. can be a wonderful country in many ways, but let's not forget that other countries can be wonderful in many ways as well."

I put away the leftovers, rinsed off the dishes, and put them in the dishwasher, while Jaime made and served the coffee. When we finally sat down again, I resumed the conversation.

"Back to our discussion," I prodded. "In the U.S. we believe in recognizing people based on *merit*. None of those 'brother-in-law' deals they do in Latin countries."

"In Peru we believe in hiring people and companies we *know*; otherwise how can we trust that they'll do a good job? Would you hire someone you didn't even *know* over someone you *knew and trusted*, just because the stranger gave you a *lower bid*? I don't think so. You'd wind up paying a lot *more* in the end. There are a lot of dishonest people who will run off with the money and leave the job half-started."

"In the U.S. we have *lawyers* to take care of that. If things aren't fair, we *sue!*"

"In Peru we know that lawsuits make money for the lawyers, but rarely solve anything."

He had me there, but I brushed that aside. "The U.S. prides itself as being the land of *opportunity*. Anyone who works hard, no matter who their parents were or the color of their skin has an equal chance. Not like Peru, where whites seem to have the upper hand."

"Really? I see the same thing in the U.S. where everyone *might* have an equal chance – unless they're black – or brown."

"You have a point there. When I was growing up in the 1950s-60s, we *did* have separate schools and restaurants," I recalled, vaguely.

"And water fountains. And blacks had to sit in the back of the bus and give up their seats to whites. The south was also infamous for its lynchings. The pot can't call the kettle black."

"I concede. But we integrated Texas schools in 1966, although it did cause a *lot* of problems. Besides," I said, quickly changing the subject, "we're not talking about the U.S. here. Peru doesn't even believe in *equal opportunity* in education, does it? How fair is it for parents to keep their children in *private* schools? That leaves the public schools without funds to educate the kids from poorer families. Besides, in Peru you don't even let boys and girls go to the same *school*. And they make everyone wear *uniforms*!" I raised my hands for emphasis.

"In Lima, boys and girls can attend classes together in places like the Roosevelt School. That's where most of the kids from the U.S. go. Personally, I found it a lot easier to go to an all-boys' school. Uniforms solve the problem of what to wear. It costs less in the long run. You have to understand, many people who go to public schools in Peru don't even come out reading or writing well. On the other hand, in Lima's private schools students can take all their classes in Spanish, English, German, or Italian if they want. By the time a student graduates high school, he's pretty fluent in a foreign language."

While pondering the thought of attending school in another *language,* my concentration was broken by a loud "Bing." The washer had finished its cycle. I jumped up to put the clothes in the dryer.

Sitting back down again to my cold coffee, I continued, "Something that's always bothered me is that in the U.S. having money is supposed to bring respect, but people who've just come into a lot of money can be so crass."

Jaime responded, "In Peru it's very hard to become rich quickly. Amassing a legitimate fortune can take generations. Peruvian businesses and government are managed by descendants of old European families. They've traveled and studied internationally and speak multiple languages, and they know how to work in various cultures. They pass their international perspective, and their businesses, from one generation to another. We believe that people with influence should have some level of culture, dress conservatively, be able to handle social situations, patronize the arts, and help those less fortunate, especially their employees."

"In *our* country we believe all men are created *equal*," I gave Jaime a wide smile.

"Except the blacks and the Catholics. When I got to Texas I found out that a lot of people here dislike Catholics. How can that be? Everyone I grew up with was Catholic. We wouldn't trust anyone who wasn't." He paced the floor.

"Well, we like Catholics. We even elected Kennedy as *president*."

He spun around to face me. "Yeah, sure. Someone *killed* him, too!"

Ouch.

Jaime was on a roll, continuing with, "In the U.S. the 'almighty dollar' rules. Capitalism is intermingled with Christianity. How can people feel self-righteous just because they go to church and listen to someone preaching about Jesus? What did *Jesus* have to do with *Capitalism*?"

I thought for a minute, and then remembered, "It wasn't Jesus, but Protestantism. Remember the 'Protestant work ethic'? I didn't see a lot of *that* in Peru."

"That's probably because there are hardly any Protestants in Peru," Jaime said, then quickly changed the subject. "Which brings me to something else I don't understand. Why do your movies always have to show sex and violence together? What do they have to do with each other?"

"I've always wondered that. I think it's led to a lot more violence in families. I can speak from direct experience in my first marriage. Won't make that mistake again. But we're not the only ones – lots of Latin men beat their wives."

"I beg your pardon?"

"You know, in the movies Latin men are so hot blooded: lying, cheating, and running around," I retorted.

"Is that what you think about *me*?" now Jaime was really feeling offended.

"Oh, not *you*. You're different."

"And my family and friends?"

"No, not them either." It was clear that I'd lost that one, so I quickly changed the subject. "Latin women are so beautiful and *sexy*. No wonder men in the U.S. think they're *loose*." Oops, I'd hit a nerve.

"*What?* In Peru, when we saw a *gringa*, we truly believed she was an easy target and that she was after only one thing. You should have heard the guys talk!"

"I beg your pardon. I'm a woman from the U.S. and I'm no pushover."

"I wasn't talking about you. I was talking about *generic gringas*. At Southwest Texas I briefly dated a Strutter. She looked so cute, shaking those pom poms and wiggling that little skirt."

"Well, what about me? I am no Strutter," I said defensively. "I was raised in a very strict family. I began to sew when I was five and by junior high was making all my own clothes. Mother taught us well. Then I majored in Home Economics because men in *our* country *value* women who can cook and sew and keep a nice house."

"With all due respect, when I was growing up, the people we associated with didn't look for the same qualities in their *wives* that they did in their *maids*."

Ouch again.

He continued, "My mother sent my sisters to cooking school and trained them in how to put on dinners, manage employees, entertain, and carry on a decent conversation. And it helps if they can play bridge."

"So, if you think so little of women in the U.S., why did you want to date me?"

"Well... remember that day when I saw you at Jiffy Lube? You had on those shiny, black short-shorts and that cut-off turquoise knit top spray-painted with a rainbow and your name across your chest?"

"I beg your pardon? I'd just finished swimming forty laps!"

"Yeah and you were in pretty good shape too!"

"So you dated me for my shiny black shorts?"

"Well, not exactly. I'd seen you around work too."

"OK, I'll choose to take that as a compliment. Now, back to bridge... I was raised that playing games, *especially* cards, was just plain *wrong*. It kept people from doing constructive work. People who played games didn't have time to take care of their families. I remember a group of women in our town who got together and played bridge every Tuesday – and drank *sherry!* They were the talk of the town."

"Wouldn't be of any interest at all to our friends in Lima."

"Speaking of drinking, what's the legal drinking age in Peru?"

"We don't have one."

"*What*? When do kids begin to drink?"

"Usually they take a sip or two at home during dinner. They learn moderation in all forms from their parents. I never found drinking very interesting until I came to college in the U.S. What we'd always taken for granted suddenly became something really radical to do." He continued, "What never made sense to me were 'dry' counties. At the university, some guys I knew were killed driving to the liquor store on the county line."

"But, doesn't not having a drinking age encourage more kids to become alcoholics?" I questioned.

"I've seen more people with drinking problems in the U.S. than in Peru, although there are people with that problem everywhere."

I couldn't let Jaime win, so I continued on: "In the U.S. we encourage our kids to become *independent*. It could be the single most important aspect of child rearing. When children graduate from high school, they go away for college, and even further away afterward."

"Sure, then the kids marry someone their parents don't even *know* and leave them all alone in their old age. That's not what I call *family values*. In Lima, families in the same social circle know each other. When their children begin to date, they can better predict whether the marriage will work out. We believe that old expression, 'Like produces like'."

"But after the kids move out, how do their parents even know who they are dating?"

"You're not paying attention. In Peru they *don't* move out. In all levels of Peruvian society, single people live in their parents' home until they marry. Besides, if they lived elsewhere, how would they save up money for a house? They'd be in debt for years."

"As you well know, in the U.S. we get 20- and 30-year loans, then slowly pay them off."

"And all that time you could have been saving money for your kids' education, a car, or your retirement instead of paying all that interest."

"Yeah, but in the U.S., we can retire at 55! What do you say to that?" I boasted.

"It's not in the U.S. It's in our *company* that people can retire at 55. People working for our company in other countries can probably do the same, perhaps at a higher percentage of their salaries. It varies all over the place." Jaime clarified. "But I know that our retirement situation will be the envy of my Peruvian friends. Peruvian law keeps people from retiring until they are 65."

But Jaime wasn't defeated yet, "Take another topic; look at your U.S. weddings. You don't even include your *families*."

"You mean in the *vows*?" Now he was questioning U.S. marriage ceremonies and I was beginning to feel a little hot under the collar.

"No, in Peru our vows are the same. I'm talking about all those bridesmaids and groomsmen."

"What's wrong with *that*? After all, they're our *close friends*. Friends are *very* important to us."

"And your friends are more important than your *family?* Are they going to be around longer than your *family*?"

"Of course not. Why do you say that?"

"Well, in Peru, instead of all those bridesmaids and groomsmen, the *parents* of the couple stand up beside the bride and groom."

"And why are they there?"

"To show their approval of the marriage."

"You mean that you have to have your *parents'* approval?"

"You do if you want to maintain family relationships. To us that is extremely important."

"But how do they do that if the couple moves away?"

"They don't usually move away. In fact, after the children are born, the *consuegras* share responsibility for managing the nannies whenever the mother needs a break."

"Well, in the U.S. we don't have that problem. I've never even met a nanny. Besides, what's a *consuegra*?"

"See what I mean? You can tell a lot about a country's value system by their language. In English, you don't even have a *word* for that important relationship. I guess if you did, you'd call it 'co-mother-in-laws'."

"What if they live in different cities than their children?"

"You aren't listening: they don't. That's a major advantage to a small country. All important business takes place in the capital. Educated people are in business, many owning or managing their own companies. I don't know how people in the U.S. handle it. Everything is too big and spread out."

"But what about those people who owned *haciendas* or mines?"

"They had homes near their work, but also maintained a home in Lima. I remember our family's *hacienda*, Rontoy, run in my father's generation by my great-uncle. It was so beautiful. When I was a kid we'd go there and run around in the countryside. My father says that when he went to college in Germany his boat landed in Hamburg. He felt so far from home. But on the dock were bails of cotton labeled 'Rontoy'."

"So the family had a *hacienda*? You've never talked about it."

"It's a sad story. Rontoy was located a couple of hours north of Lima, near the town of Huara, the place where Peru declared its independence from Spain. It is said that the liberator, Jose San Martin, spent the night at Rontoy, riding to Huara the next day to proclaim independence."

"So they grew cotton at Rontoy..."

"And sugar cane. They even had a small electricity generation plant, installed by my great-uncle, Jorge, who started *Empresas Eléctricas*, the Peruvian electric company. I wonder if that plant is still there. You see, that whole way of life was destroyed by President Velasco's Agrarian Reform while I was in college."

"How sad. Some day I'd like to visit Rontoy," I said wistfully.

"Oh, I haven't been back there since the takeover. Agrarian Reform almost bankrupted Peru. You know the old theory: 'Take from the rich and give to the poor.' It sounds good, but in Peru there was no transition period. It happened when the crops were ready for harvest. From one day to the next, the hired hands were supposed to intuitively know how to grow crops, harvest them, transport them, and market them domestically and internationally. But they could barely read and write! The *hacienda* owners moved to Lima and sold most of their other assets to repay the banks for the seeds. It destroyed the economy of Peru as well as the entire country's food supply. Before that day, Peru's economy was as strong as Japan's. After Agrarian Reform, it became one of the poorest countries on Earth. Many years later, some of our family visited Rontoy. They were met by the man who kept the horses. He cried and asked, 'Why did you abandon us?' He couldn't comprehend that it was the *government* who did it." My eyes began to water.

The dryer buzzed loudly. I took a deep breath, wiped my eyes, and ran to pull the clothes out before they wrinkled; being fully aware that all the time I was performing tasks every middle- and upper-class Peruvian family paid a maid to do. After the wash, there were carpets to vacuum and floors to mop. Yes, I was a successful U.S. business woman doing the work of a Latin American maid. Granted, the middle class might have only part-time maids and didn't play bridge, but the irony of my life was still apparent.

I sat back down. That conversation had made me dizzy. It brought into question the superiority of my secure upbringing in a small Texas town. So many things that I always *knew* were right or wrong suddenly didn't seem so black and white. Clearly, there were good arguments for another way of life; one that preserved the family and the culture; one that did not result in immigrants having their names shortened and/or misspelled by impatient customs officials or civil registrars and their family histories and values lost in what we in the U.S. call the "melting pot."

That dizzy feeling would continue and sometimes even escalate over the years, as everything I knew "for sure" was called into question. I would have to build another identity, a more understanding life, a fairer life; one in which personal business achievement and national pride left me with no sense of superiority whatsoever.

Paco and Hiltrud in the back yard of the house on
Avenida Pardo in Miraflores, Lima, 1950.
(L-R), Jorge (9), Lichi (7), Tere (5), Paco (3), and in
front, Jaime (8 months).

52

"Reflections from the Patio," watercolor of the *piscinita*, by Franci P. Kelley.

4

Reflections from the Patio

"Whew, what a great meal," I exclaimed one afternoon after a delicious lunch of chicken served over fettuccini and covered with a sauce of ground pecans, ají peppers, and cream. For dessert there were slices of tree-ripened, lavender-scented Edward mangos, served over vanilla ice cream. "Think I'll just go out to the patio and take a *siesta*, OK?" I asked, only half expecting a response, as I headed directly for the long, covered swing on the terrace.

For me, a *siesta* in Lima always transcended the North American word "nap." It was not the poor excuse for a break that I had made in Texas, as an exhausted corporate employee. No, this *siesta* was truly a delicious event, especially when enjoyed on the covered swing on my in-laws' patio in Lima.

Since we married, our goal had been to return to Lima, and to this very patio, once a year. That did not always happen, but this was one of those fortunate days when I was able to temporarily occupy the prized resting spot on the swinging bench. There was no schedule for this *siesta*, nor was anything else planned that afternoon. I would have much rather spent the time with Hiltrud, but she passed away years ago. After reclining, I quickly fell asleep, and dreamt of Hiltrud, gone from our sight, but never, ever from our hearts.

I found the perfect mother-in-law when I was almost forty years old. Hiltrud Sehr was born in Aschaffenburg in southern Germany. Engineering studies took my father-in-law, Paco, from Lima to a university in Germany. Paco met Hiltrud, a beautiful German *fräulein* with dark hair and brown eyes, when he rented a room from her mother. Their relationship was just beginning to develop when Hitler invaded Poland and changed their world forever. There was no time to delay decisions. As soon as Paco got his degree in Electro-Mechanical Engineering, he and Hiltrud decided to marry as quickly as possible and leave Germany. Because she married a foreigner during wartime, the Nazi government stripped Hiltrud of her German citizenship. Paco and Hiltrud left the country by escaping over the Alps into France. They waited in seclusion for weeks before they could find passage on a ship headed for New York City. When they arrived, passing the Statue of Liberty, they stayed for weeks with one of Paco's wealthy uncles, who treated them to the best that New York had to offer, buying Hiltrud a new wardrobe. But in a couple of weeks they had to catch another ship to Lima. As they crossed the Panama Canal, Hiltrud marveled at a boatful of fruit she had only seen in photos – pineapple. She would become familiar with this and a score of other tropical fruits in her new-found country. Hiltrud arrived in Lima at age eighteen, speaking not a word of Spanish and knowing nothing of the Latin customs.

"I found a Spanish translation of 'Gone with the Wind'," she once told me. "It was so long that by the time I finished it, I felt at home with the language."

Hiltrud would never again see her only sister, Elizabeth Sehr, who they called "little one" or "Mädi" in German. Mädi was killed one night when Allied forces, returning from an attack on a Nazi armament factory, dropped their left-over bombs on the innocent residents of Darmstadt. The next morning, her mother combed the still-liquid asphalt streets, finally identifying Mädi's body by the imprint of a white-gold ring with a small square diamond. When Hiltrud's mother went in search of coffins, there were none left in the town. Hiltrud's only brother, George, lost a leg on the Russian front, but unlike many in his battalion, returned to Germany alive, to spend the rest of his life documenting his hate for the Third Reich. Years later, when Hiltrud's mother visited Peru, her behavior was erratic and her eyes were wild; the trauma and atrocities of the war had driven her mad.

During her first ten years in Lima, Hiltrud gave birth to five children. The oldest was Jorge, followed by Isabel (Lichi), afterward Teresa (Tere), then José Francisco (Paco), and the youngest, my wonderful husband, Jaime. As she matured, Hiltrud's brown hair turned to silver, and she wore it simply but elegantly in a short pageboy. Though she lived among the Peruvian upper class, Hiltrud wore simple tailored blouses and skirts, with almost no makeup. I especially remember her large hands wrinkled with age and work, and her manicured fingernails. Instead of a wedding ring, Hiltrud always wore a thin platinum band with an enormous pearl that she would rub when she was tense. Unlike Peruvian women, Hiltrud often worked alongside her maids. She not only learned the Peruvian customs, but excelled in them so well that admiring friends and family continue to recount their love for her years after her death. Hiltrud was lovely – highly intelligent, yet gentle and well-spoken in German, Spanish, and English. She was an elegant hostess, the perfect listener, a peace maker, and resolute in keeping her family close together. She made herself so easy to love.

I still clearly remember my first trip to Lima following Hiltrud's death. I was working at the English secretary desk on the upstairs landing when the grandfather clock next to me stopped abruptly. As the family discussed how to wind it up, we were simultaneously drawn towards a small upper left-hand drawer of the English secretary, located next to the clock. When we opened the drawer, there was the clock-winding key, attached by a thin, red satin ribbon to a message. In Spanish it read:

"It is better to get life out of your years than years out of your life." Hiltrud must have known that someone else would have to wind the clock in the future.

Back there on the patio in 1995, falling asleep with tears in my eyes, I began dreaming of the first time I met Hiltrud – before I ever came to Lima. It was in 1987, after midnight on a hot and stormy Texas summer night. Jaime and I had rented a house on Surfside beach, south of Houston, so my in-laws-to-be and I could get to know each other. What I knew from my years in Mexico was that, if they did not accept me, Jaime and I would never marry. This family, no matter how far apart they lived, was too closely knit to endure another marriage to a difficult *gringa*.

Jaime went to the airport to meet the Lima flight. I was left with our "Brady Bunch" of four. There was Elisa, my daughter, who had thick, cascading dark-brown hair, fair skin, and big brown eyes. At seventeen, she was smart, cocky, and rebellious. She usually insisted on having the last word. Next in age was Pati, fourteen years old and Jaime's oldest child. She was thin but well-toned, with light-blonde hair, and blue eyes. Pati was always the peace maker, carefully weighing every word and everyone else's feelings before speaking, which meant that she didn't get to talk much. Then came Kristy, who was just ten months younger than Pati. She was taller than the others, had curly medium-blonde hair, blue-green eyes, and was always full of unspent energy. The youngest was Jaime Carlos, or JC as we called him. At age eight, JC was short and pudgy, his full lips and mischievous bright blue eyes giving away that he both loved food and hated teenage girls. He dedicated himself to tormenting them.

A terrible storm was brewing on the Gulf. It had begun at sunset and had moved in with the dark. The winds were so high that we struggled for half an hour in the rain to bring our things upstairs and into the house.

Paco and Hiltrud's flight was late, so by the time Jaime arrived with his parents it was close to midnight. Hearing the car doors open, I left the kids upstairs in their beds and ran down the outside staircase to meet them. Exhausted after their day-long journey, they were soaked through by the pouring rain, their clothes whipped around their bodies by the violent winds. As we were introduced, Hiltrud put her hands on my shoulders and looked directly into my eyes. She stood there saying nothing, and then she smiled broadly, covering me with kisses and hugs. My grateful tears, mixed with the raindrops, washed away all apprehension. She was the embodiment of love itself.

In the week that followed, we shared recipes and stories, all in Spanish. I learned a new word, *quizá*, which Hiltrud explained to me meant "perhaps." Yes, perhaps I would someday become part of this wonderful family. Just perhaps. And indeed, I did.

Hiltrud imagined a better future, but she would not live to see it. Soon after she and Paco returned from their Texas visit, the Peruvian economy began to crumble and the terrorist attacks worsened. *Sendero Luminoso* terrorists had surrounded the capital, cutting off the electricity and food supplies. One night, just after midnight, when we finally got through on the phone, I could hear bombs going off. As we finished our conversation, I mastered the courage to extend a heart-felt invitation to Jaime's parents.

"Remember that at *any time* you are welcome to come live with us."

There was a long silence on the other end of the line. Then, over the sound of bombs destroying near-by electrical towers, Hiltrud very wisely and kindly replied to me,

"And you remember that, at any time, *you* are welcome to come live with *us*."

We would never live together with Jaime's parents, on either side of the equator. Just months after our conversation, Hiltrud was in Lima, writing in her daily journal, when the pen slipped from her fingers, drawing a jagged line down the page. She got up from her desk and her shoe fell off, but she didn't feel it. Hiltrud immediately went to her doctor, whose tests revealed that she had a fast-growing brain tumor. Jaime and I were in Europe at the time on a two-week vacation. When we left, everyone had been in perfect health. Upon reaching Florence, we called home to find that Hiltrud had been flown to New York for treatment at Columbia-Presbyterian Neurological Center. Their diagnosis was brain cancer which was visibly advancing every day.

We immediately left Florence and rushed back to Paris, where we caught the next flight to New York, arriving in time to hold Hiltrud's hand, say goodbye, and exchange last hugs. I remember assuring Hiltrud that we'd fly down to Lima soon for a visit. Her answer was once again, "*Quizá.*" Perhaps we would see each other again. Perhaps not.

Then we flew back to Texas, hoping for a miracle. We immediately developed the photos of our last visit together and were devastated to find that, in every one, Hiltrud's face was a blur – even though everyone else in the photo was in perfect focus.

The sad phone call came less than a week later. We rushed to the Houston airport, arriving in Lima about midnight. But we were too late.

The family had followed Peruvian custom, burying Hiltrud earlier that day.

I cried and cried, "She's gone forever!" But was that really true?

Growing up in WWII Germany, Hiltrud learned first-hand how fleeting a country's wealth and power can be. She saw how personal security could evaporate with one bombing raid. By losing hers, she learned how fragile families are. By leaving her homeland, she knew what it felt like to be an outsider. In a new land, with a new culture and another language, Hiltrud fought a different kind of battle – not with guns or hatred, but with her love – to keep her family together. And even in her death, she won. Hiltrud could see through languages, cultures, religions, and trends. I was wrong – she wasn't gone forever. Hiltrud lives on in the lessons she had passed on to her children, her friends, and to me. She was both a true matriarch and a true citizen of the world. I loved her dearly.

I awoke from my patio nap with a start, realizing that I had been lost in a dreamscape of memories. Rubbing my eyes, I decided to savor the landscape in front of me as well. I looked down, examining the patio floor, which extended from the dining room on the right, with its extensive *mampara* sliding tempered glass wall, past the living room in front of me, the wall of which was also a *mampara*. The patio was floored with somewhat chipped terracotta tiles, baked black and covered with decades-worth of wax. The wooden pergola was completely covered by a large, peach-colored bougainvillea, which cascaded down the sides, gently touching the top of the window of the study to the extreme left. The swinging bench on which I dozed was set under the pergola and shaded by those flowers.

Also under the pergola was a large rustic wooden table and matching chairs. Alongside this was a wooden drink cart in the shape of a small wheel barrow, lovingly made many years ago by my father-in-law, Paco. At that time he was head of Volkswagen Peru, but that never stopped him from taking time out for his woodworking projects.

Near the pergola were a grill and a serving table that brought to mind many delicious meals enjoyed with the family. Beyond that, on the grass, were a half dozen *tumbonas* (recliners) where we enjoyed the intense equatorial sun.

The patio was surrounded by high brick and concrete walls painted white, alongside which grew tall eucalyptus trees and bushes full of bright orange and lilac flowers. Below that were rare hibiscus bushes in colors ranging from snowy white to hot pink to the deepest royal shade of violet. They were a tribute to Hiltrud, who personally cared for them for decades, during humid years as well as years of drought. And, as always, singing canaries and beautiful hummingbirds filled the air. In the summer there were super-size bumble bees, so large I could actually *hear* them inhale and exhale as they buzzed from flower to flower. Because there is no rain in Lima, every garden was a testimony to the caretaker, and this garden was truly a work of love. After Hiltrud's swift and involuntary departure from this earth six years before, loyal gardeners continued to maintain these beautiful plants in her memory.

Turning around in the direction of the yard, my eyes focused on the *piscinita*, the small swimming pool outside the dining room window to the right. For decades it was the center of family gatherings. Long before I ever visited Peru, I saw a collection of videos of this family home and the eleven grandchildren, now young adults, bathing in and playing around this very pool. The pool water, which only on the sunniest days might be somewhat hotter, was usually below 60 degrees Fahrenheit, requiring a great deal of bravery before entering, and no one stayed in for very long.

Since its construction in 1968, this patio had been the venue for family gatherings every Saturday afternoon. But today, the first day of autumn, the patio and the *piscinita* sat still and alone. In my reflections, I could almost hear the happy voices of times gone by and return to those beautiful, lazy summer days – so long ago it seemed – when I was invited to join this huge and loving family, to eat on this patio, and bathe in this pool.

I looked back toward the house and through the sliding glass *mamparas*, and saw Paco, a great man now in the winter of his years, slumped in a wheelchair. I somehow knew that this would be the last time that I would see Jaime's father before he was reunited with Hiltrud. When this occurred, everything that was before me would change. I could not help but cry.

Santa Rosa and the Virgin Mary looked down from the huge religious oils that adorned the interior walls. They assured me that while Paco's death would signify the end of an era, it would not be the end of the family. The passing of this woman, this man, and this house would be only one point in time in the great road that is eternity.

Adiós querido patio; adiós verano. Goodbye dear patio; goodbye summer. When I see you again it will be winter and after that you may be no more. But for now I will inhale your fragrance and capture this delicious moment to keep in my heart – forever.

Paco did meet Hiltrud on the other side not long afterward, but Jaime and I were not there to see him off. I was in Barcelona on the first day of a multi-week European business trip; Jaime was working in Texas. The rest of the family was in Lima, at his side. They said they understood our predicament. But how could they, when we ourselves did not think it was permissible to miss the death of a parent. I began to understand how painful Jaime's life must have been all those years; living and raising a family in the U.S. while all the time being part of his close family in Peru.

I vowed that just as soon as we were able we would spend more time in Lima. At the time, I had no way of knowing what that would mean. I only knew that fair is fair and that the legacy so lovingly created by Paco and Hiltrud deserved to be kept alive and nurtured. By bringing more of my life to Lima, I could help do that. Besides, I had fallen in love: first with Jaime, then the family, and increasingly, with Peru itself.

5

Quest for the Mary Virgin

The Texas coastal night is calm and humid and the spring air is filled with sounds of crickets chirping. I am alone, sitting cross-legged on a blood-red and navy Persian rug on the floor of our foyer, staring lovingly at a large oil painting of a woman and two cherubs. I still do not believe that we own this beautiful work of art, this loving Madonna human-saint.

The work is a large religious oil, painted in the Peruvian Colonial-style by Lima artist Rubén Aponte. In it, a woman descending from the clouds is delicately balanced on a sliver of a moon. Her sapphire and crimson cape is blowing in the wind, revealing the long white gown of *La Inmaculada*. Both the cape and the gown are richly accented in intricate gold filigree. On her head is a golden crown with jewels, and around the crown a halo made from a circle of twelve stars. In her hair is a golden clasp that seems to draw its power from the sun's rays pouring out from behind her body, passing on to her a Divine source of energy. Her face is more Renaissance Italian than a traditional stylized Latin Madonna. Wherever I move, she is watching me, with her sweet, Mona Lisa-like smile.

Surrounding this serene beauty are the symbols of the Mary litany: seat of wisdom, house of gold, morning star, fountain of virtue, mirror of justice, vessel of devotion and honor, and portal to heaven. They remind me that this is not just any woman. The painting is framed in a large, ornate, hand-carved wooden frame that is overlaid with bronze leaf, *pan de bronce*. A more celestial Mary would be hard to find.

At her feet, just beneath the sliver of moon, are two rather impatient-looking cherubs gazing up with bored stares, as if they just wish she would "get on with" whatever she is doing. I could stare at this painting for hours. Somewhere in those loving eyes I find strength and focus for my ever-changing life.

Upon entering the foyer, people who visit our home often comment on what, by all rights, should be in the sanctuary of a Roman Catholic Church. Most people gasp momentarily, commenting on its quality. Pre-teens have been known to ask how much it is worth, as if we might have bought her as an investment. The most apropos response we've received was from an artist friend of ours who saw her, stepped back startled, and exclaimed, "Holy Mother of God!"

When our family of six left for Peru in mid-December 1993, we had no intention of acquiring another painting. We only took our "painting carrying case" along because some day some family member might want to bring a painting to someone. Jaime and his father had made the large, wooden painting case to protect a *Pachamama* (mother earth) painting we had brought back to commemorate his mother's death.

We arrived in Lima after midnight. It was the end of an eleven-hour trip that seemed much longer. We were overjoyed to see our family again. In spite of their work schedules the next day, most of the family had expectantly waited outside the airport in the chilly wind for the return of the U.S. contingent of their family to their *real* homeland, Peru. When Jaime's brother Jorge noticed the painting box, he jumped to the conclusion that we were going to bring back another painting.

"How could we?" we chimed in unison, "Our walls are already covered with Peruvian paintings. We're only bringing this box down for *someone else's* convenience."

Not easily dissuaded, Jorge mentioned that he had met a wonderful painter. "How nice," we said, as we thought of how much nicer any bed would look right now. We are not sure exactly how it happened, but sometime during the ride home from the airport we agreed that we would visit Jorge's new-found talent the next day – in the afternoon.

Early the next morning, Jorge called to say that he was picking us up for a visit to meet Rubén. "Who?" we asked blankly.

"The painter I mentioned last night," Jorge replied, "He is painting a marvelous Adoration of the Magi for me. Perhaps you'll want him to paint something for you."

"Oh no!" the kids wailed, "Not *another* one of those paintings. Our house already looks like a Catholic church! What are we going to do with all that stuff when you *die*?"

Ignoring the kid's complaints and not planning on dying any time soon, I inquired, "Is his house far?"

"Not too far," Jorge explained. "It's in old Surco, on the way to Barranco."

Barranco is a dreamy old town where Lima's wealthiest once built their beach retreat mansions. Today Barranco has been annexed into the city of Lima. Many of the old mansions have been turned into clubs; a haven for the young and the musical. I loved going to Barranco – during the day.

Surco is a district adjacent to Barranco. Its southern tip never had the beauty or wealth of its neighboring district, though it was once famous for its Pisco, the clear brandy that is the national beverage of

Peru. Today south Surco looks like just another run-down section of any major Latin American city.

No one could have prepared me for the journey to Rubén's house, although my years in Guadalajara did help a bit. We backed out onto the heavily-trafficked thoroughfare in front of the house. The roads were dusty and bumpy. Along the route we passed numerous impromptu carpenter shops, as well as muffler and car repair garages. Vendors hawked little bags of artichoke hearts on the street corners. Dodging belching, erratically swerving buses, we passed a billboard which read, "Elephant shocks, for the roads of Peru." I wagered they sold a lot of them.

I don't know how we navigated. Turns were erratic, with frequent Z- and U-turns. Street signs had been stolen and traffic lights broken. Traffic jams pressed cars so tightly together that Jorge banged his hand on the door of a car pressing in on his driver's side. In the opposite lane a truck full of adolescent soldiers, in fatigues and carrying submachine guns, glided past expensive homes with explosions of pink and red bougainvillea spilling over their high protective walls. An evangelical church on the left displayed a large sign in Spanish proclaiming, "Jesus is the same yesterday, today, and always."

But is He present? I wondered. *How can Jesus be in a place like this?*

Just then I heard a "crunch." A Volvo had hit us, cracking our driver's side rear-view mirror, but nobody was willing, or brave enough, to stop to discuss it. Buses as well as cars cut in front of us without signaling. Then we got stuck in a traffic jam between six belching buses and an old minivan. The air was suffocating.

"I'll turn on the air conditioning," Jaime offered. Ah, relief at last! But traffic wasn't moving, so the engine overheated. He turned off the AC and we resumed sweating.

We passed a military zone with signs in large red letters, which translated roughly warned, "Don't hang around here or we'll shoot!" A tank on the left was surrounded by black sandbags. On either side we saw men with machine guns ensconced in soot-covered concrete gun towers.

We drove through a large open-air market occupying both lanes of the street, then made a 120-degree right turn, almost colliding with an abandoned vegetable truck in the middle of the street. As if on cue, Dodges and Chevys from decades past whizzed by, held together with Duct Tape and Bond-O. We drove through broken glass, then edged left past concrete boulders blocking off the street. We wound past an old church and onto an equally blocked street with a small market, where we saw a small cinnamon-skinned man with rumpled clothes and a cap.

"There's Rubén's father!" Jorge pointed ahead. "He's usually leaning against the wall, so he's a good landmark."

We hired someone to guard our car, trying not to stare at the chickens being strangled and hung up for sale on the sidewalk – exactly two feet in front of Rubén's front door.

"Watch your step. There's blood," Jaime cautioned.

We tapped on the termite-eaten turquoise doors, gently for fear they'd fall off. Rubén answered the door and asked us to step two feet down into his studio. In the U.S. the word "studio" evokes visions of white walls and streaming sunlight. Not so in Rubén's studio. Like all houses in Latin countries, the walls were made of brick, covered with plaster and painted. These walls were painted with chipping blue and sometimes chipping golden-yellow paint. The floors were a collage of broken hand-painted tile.

Rubén invited us to sit on an old upholstered couch with broken springs, covered with old sheets. On the other side of the room were a refrigerator and another old couch. At the other end of the studio was a door leading to the rest of Rubén's house. The 12-foot high ceiling with exposed beams was covered with yellowed, peeling paper. The hole in the roof was plugged with newspaper.

"I take out the newspaper to get natural light for my paintings," Rubén explained.

I stepped out the door to check on our car, just in time to see a new chicken dangling upside down with its throat slit, shaking violently as it bled to death. I began to feel a little queasy, and decided it was better to step back inside. As my eyes adjusted to the poorly lit room, they fell on the Adoration of the Magi, the painting Rubén was making for Jorge. Still unfinished, it was easily a yard square and painted in exquisite detail. Of particular interest was the face of one of the kings. That face was so good it could be admired in any museum, anywhere. A lustful urgency began to overtake me. Perhaps someday in the distant future, we too might possess a work of art as fine as this one.

Then my eyes turned back to study Rubén. Who was this obviously talented and yet still humble artist? Rubén was, at that time, 39 years old, about 5' 8" with cinnamon-colored skin, a short mane of shiny black hair, and brilliant black eyes hooded with heavy black brows. The first time we saw Rubén he was wearing a soccer shirt, jeans, and black tennis shoes – the same attire he wore on all subsequent visits. In talking with Rubén he told us that he was an avid soccer player and played soccer every Sunday, no matter what painting he was working on.

We found out that Rubén grew up in this neighborhood and went to the famous Bellas Artes art institute in Lima.

"When I graduated, I was so poor that I couldn't buy brushes, so I made them from my own hair. For a while I had a little dog, whose hair I'd use for special applications, but the little dog was run over," he told us sadly.

"How did the homemade brushes work?" we inquired.

"About as well as these do," he replied with a smile, holding up two commercially-produced brushes.

In talking to Jorge, we found out that Rubén was already well known, but his artwork was not commercially available. His paintings were commissioned and could be found in homes and churches in Lima, in the U.S., Canada, Central America, Venezuela, Colombia, Austria, and in both a museum and homes in Spain. As with so many artists, his paintings traveled where he could not. Rubén's greatest dream was to travel around Europe to see the works of the famous Continental masters.

It was a shame that Rubén didn't have the commercial organization behind him that his famous namesake had enjoyed in Belgium, where his students painted most of the piece, leaving the great artist to finish only a few of the details. On the other hand, this modern-day Rubén had a quality control that the Belgian Rubens did not. Every stroke of this Rubén's works was painted by him and him alone.

So, back to the painting that we had not yet dared to think of...

When we inquired about the inspiration for Rubén's artwork, he pointed to an unkempt collection of prints on a 1950s style dinette. Those prints favored classic Peruvian artists, both famous and obscure, but also included works of well-known European artists. The partially-finished oils hanging on the studio walls demonstrated that Rubén could paint an incredible range of artistic styles.

"So how," I asked Jorge in English, "does one decide on what to ask Rubén to paint?"

Jorge explained in Spanish, "What most of the customers do is select a painting style they like and then ask Rubén to change specific details, since hardly anyone really likes everything about a painting. For example, you might like a Madonna, but not like the figures around her, her robes, her face, or the background. So you tell Rubén what to altar and he does it. He can paint anything in oil. *Anything.*"

"So I could have *exactly* the painting I want?" I asked starry-eyed. The seed had planted itself in my psyche. I envisaged a painting of a Madonna descending from the clouds, her blue cape with gold-filigree flowing in the heavenly breeze, with charming cherubs at her feet. Until that moment, it had just been a fantasy. But the seed in my mind began to germinate. If we acted with haste, it just might be possible to commission the painting of my dreams and take it home with us on this very trip! I knew I was in trouble when I started pouring through Rubén's prints, looking for the closest painting I could find to what I wanted.

When I was just about to give up, at the bottom of the collection was a crude model of the painting of my dreams. It was the basic style I wanted, except I wanted a more realistic face and hands, more flowing robes, and more gold filigree. The angels at the Madonna's feet just had to go. The ones in the print looked like they were looking up her gown and, to top it all off, were actually quite ugly creatures. That would never do! Besides, the whole painting would be just too formal. I decided to inject a slice of reality into our painting by substituting in two decidedly bored cherubs, originally painted by Raphael. OK, so they were from a famous painting, but they were without doubt my favorite cherubs. This was going to be our painting, wasn't it? And so was born the idea for The Mary Litany, who I privately referred to as our Mary Virgin.

After talking these ideas over with Jaime, Jorge, and Rubén, we decided to commission the painting. Everything was settled now, except for a few details, like the finished size, the price, and the small matter of completion date.

For the size, we measured the painting box. No use in getting a magnificent work of art on a small canvas. The box measured 22" x 35", so we chose that size. When we got home we'd find a wall for it, we were sure. Now to the delicate matter of price. Paintings in Peru are still far less expensive than their stateside counterparts, but they are by no means free. Commissioning a painting directly from the artist would guarantee him a higher asking price and us a lower purchase price by cutting out the art dealer, who often keep the names of their artists as well-guarded secrets. Rubén stated his price and, although we gulped, we accepted it without bargaining.

In the weeks that followed, we visited our Lady Madonna and Rubén six more times. With each visit the painting became more real. Of particular interest were the visits coinciding with Christmas and New Year's Eve, when the already crowded streets became virtually impossible to navigate. With each visit we doubted more and more that the painting would ever be completed and dry by our departure date.

By New Year's Eve, our printing was almost finished. Rubén was working on the elaborate gold filigree on Mary's gown. Having anticipated that this would be our last visit, we had purchased a bottle of champagne to share with Rubén and his wife, Señora María. During that final visit we sat for two hours as Rubén finished up the last little bit of filigree on the Virgin's cape. When he was finished at last, we all stood back to marvel at the creation and to toast the artist.

There she was with her gold filigreed gown flowing in the wind, her delicate hands pressed prayerfully near her beautiful Renaissance face. At her feet were the Raphael angels, looking as bored and yet as lovely as ever. If there was a dry eye in the room, I didn't see it. Now it was time for more tears, as we separated the creation from the creator.

"How could we be so cruel," I thought. "How can someone sell his creations, his 'children', for money?"

We took the Virgin down from the easel and gently laid her in the box. We bid Rubén and Señora Maria *adiós*, promising to take care of his "child," displaying her in a place of dignity, and treating her with respect. And we promised to always remember Rubén and his wonderful talent.

That night, on the floor of the family home, Jaime spent hours carefully packing our Virgin so she wouldn't be damaged in shipping. At dinner we all raised our glasses in a toast to her and then closed and sealed the box.

On the long flight home we had many anxious moments as we strained to see how the baggage handlers were treating our newest family member. When we finally arrived home the next day, we unpacked our prize and found it just as perfect as when it was lovingly packed away, many thousands of miles before. What a relief!

So that is how the celestial was born of the venial and finally came to grace our entry hall, spreading her warmth and peace throughout our home. And whenever I look at her, I feel somehow magically lifted up to another realm of insight. That is, until the little bored cherubs at her feet bring me back to reality.

Though we did not realize it at the time, we would become patrons of religious art, as well as life-long friends of Rubén and his family. From them I would learn about bravery in the face of despair and still more about the power of a close family. I learned that real power does not lie in military might. Tanks and machine guns can never win as long as the spirit of God persists in those who have dedicated themselves to serving the Divine, regardless of the circumstances.

The Mary Litany by
Rubén Aponte, c. 1988.

In later years, Rubén and another friend and artist in Texas, Franci Kelley, collaborated on a project to create four large angel oil paintings to fit into triangular niches around the alter at our home church in Lake Jackson. As he finished the last angel, Rubén was diagnosed with, and underwent surgery and chemo for, advanced-stage cancer. As of this writing, Rubén's cancer is in remission and he has begun painting again.

In the decades since we first met Rubén, we have seen the area they live in become increasingly crowded, rundown, and dangerous. It is as if God is unfolding a perfect vision of hell on the streets, with heaven hidden behind a battered door, stretched on canvas, and in the eyes and hands of a man who continues his vision despite his environment.

Rubén in his studio, creating the Angel of Music, the first in a series of four angels that today surround the altar of St. Timothy's Episcopal in Lake Jackson, TX.

6

Rites of Passage

I arrived in Barcelona fighting jet lag, on the first day of a three-week business trip through our corporation's European chemical plants. That day in the late spring of 1996 was flawlessly clear and bright as I sat on the dark brown and grey cobblestone terrace of a small café tucked away on the city end of Las Ramblas, that broad promenade stretching from the ocean to the town center. Vendors lined the waves of green and white tile making up the famous walkway, selling everything from flowers to art to puppets. The trees, lush with fresh green leaves, swayed in the breeze to the music of street musicians, who as strange as it may seem, were from the Peruvian Andes.

Leaving Jaime for a three-week business trip tore at my heartstrings. How nice it would have been if we could have done this together. I was keenly aware that, at this perfect moment on this perfect day, I was totally alone. Eager to escape my solitude, I reviewed my options for the next day. A tour seemed to be the ideal solution for enjoying myself without risk. I finished my espresso and walked through the medieval section of town, where I encountered a small travel agency. Tour options included an out-of-town excursion to the famous monastery of Montserrat, built on a sharp outcropping of rocks. As this monastery had always held some fascination for me, I signed up.

The next day, the tour group set off in the cool morning haze. We arrived at Montserrat shortly before lunch, just in time for a church service. Before going into the church, I purchased a small red candle at an open-air stand. Heavy on my thoughts was Lima and the family there.

At that time Peru was in the first presidential term of Alan García and in the grip of 7,800 percent annual inflation. *Sendero Luminoso* terrorist attacks had killed over 25,000 people, while outbreaks of cholera had left another 18,000 dead. But closest to my heart was Jaime's father, Paco, trapped against his will in a deteriorating body while also losing his mind. Even before the Alzheimer's became so advanced, he was eager to join Hiltrud on the other shore. I lit my candle, placed it in the holder, knelt, and prayed fervently for the future of Peru and for Paco's release.

That evening, when I returned to my hotel on a park near the Diagonal, there was an urgent message to call home. When I finally got through to Jaime, he told me that his father had died that afternoon. The time of his father's death was just six hours after I lit that candle.

The problem with answered prayers is that no one can ever be sure of the timing. In this case, Jaime and I would not be able to attend Paco's funeral service because of my business trip, which was just beginning. I painfully remembered that we missed Hiltrud's funeral too, if only by just a few hours.

The family forgave us again, saying it would be best to come later to settle the estate. They would see to it that the gardener and one of Jaime's sister Teresa's trusted maids, Doris, would maintain the house until it was sold and the estate was settled. Doris was in a difficult situation, as she was pregnant with her first child and no husband in sight. The family agreed that she would need a protected environment with light work until she could get on her feet again.

By the time I returned from Europe, I was exhausted physically and mentally. Still, I felt the pull to get to Lima as soon as possible. But this was not the plan; I had another multi-week review of chemical plants in Brazil, Argentina, and Colombia.

At home in Texas, distraught and thinking about the upcoming trips, I looked out our bedroom window, through the trees and grass and towards the creek that ran through our back yard. I asked myself, "How can I make another business trip, with all that is going on in Peru?"

As if on cue, a snow-white squirrel ran down from a nearby tree and stood, pecan in hand, staring straight into my bedroom window for what seemed like several minutes. It felt like an angel, sent just for me. "Jaime, get the camera! You won't believe this."

We took several photos of that squirrel, which would reappear over a period of several *years* – always just before I left on a particularly arduous trip. Knowing that this had to be a sign, I prayed for an interpretation. The message I received was, "I am with you. You will survive." And survive I did, in time to head back to Lima a few weeks after my return from the South American tour.

We arrived in Lima in early August. This was the first time I had been there in winter and, with the terrorist situation, I was particularly uneasy about what we would encounter. During our last trip we experienced severe food shortages, lengthy blackouts, and the sound of bombs exploding in the distance while we tried to sleep. Even though four soldiers were stationed at every intersection in that part of town, the terrorists sneaked into the city by night, killed dogs, and hung them from lamp posts to scare the residents. To top it all off, there was a "once every 50 years" drought. During that visit, each family member was allocated less than two *cups* of water each a day, which we divided between bathing and flushing the toilet. How could Jaime's family survive under these worsening conditions?

The family was there to greet us at the airport. On the drive to the house on Caminos del Inca, Jorge told us that Paco and Hiltrud's beautiful multi-level home would be sold and the estate divided among the five children.

"We have decided that you two will stay in the master suite."

Sitting on Paco and Hiltrud's bed was eerie. To my left, through a long sliding glass wall, lay the manicured grass and bushes of the rose garden, still populated by the roses Hiltrud had planted decades ago. The patio to the right was smaller, with three walls of ceiling-to-floor glass and a rock floor in whose center stood a tall tree bearing bright tulip-shaped orange blossoms. Looking onto that patio, I remembered how it appeared while Hiltrud was alive, when it contained pots of white periwinkles and decorative cages of yellow and white canaries. A chilly breeze swept through my body and visions of those happy summer days burned in contrast to the grey pallor of the occasion.

The family always told me that in Lima, the 98 percent winter humidity was something that had to be experienced to be believed. As the coldest recorded temperature was 53 degrees Fahrenheit, houses were heated by only an occasional small space heater. Closets quickly collected mold if not dehumidified. The dehumidifier running in the large master bedroom closet collected over a *gallon* of water a day. But under the cover of an electric blanket, the nights were cozy and comfortable. There was, however, the persistent knowledge that we were in the bed where Paco and Hiltrud had slept – and had died. While they surely would have granted us permission, we would rather have been elsewhere.

In preparation for the auspicious and delicate matter of property division, the family had asked Tía Lucha, Jaime's paternal aunt and godmother, and a national authority on antiques, to appraise the family treasures. Jaime's brother, Paco, created a spreadsheet and gave a copy to the other brothers and sisters, asking them to mark items they were interested in. Foremost on everyone's minds was the desire to maintain the closeness of the family. Failing to do so would violate the decades of harmony so carefully masterminded by the great lady.

The morning of the division began with the gathering of the family. Present were the five brothers and sisters, their respective maids, and me, the lone spouse. The family began with a review of the spreadsheet, followed by a walk through the house, noting the items that were not listed. This was followed by several hours of estimating and by rounds of selections.

The maids, brought together for the first time in years, shared stories and laughed away the hours as they cooked in the kitchen. They took their breaks in Hiltrud's herb garden and also in the carport, under the enormous purple bougainvillea that cascaded down from the roof. They appeared at comfortable intervals to keep us supplied with coffee, tea and snacks.

I stayed with the brothers and sisters, but occupied myself with capturing the moment, as theirs was family business. I particularly remember the large white limestone fireplace, whose chimney rose to the top of the twenty-foot-high ceiling, its fire providing warmth more psychological than physical.

Looking out the sliding glass wall I surveyed the back patio with its small swimming pool, now filled with fallen yellow, red, pink, and purple hibiscus flowers. At my feet, on the other side of the glass, lay a large yellow and black striped bumblebee, slowly dying. It was symbolic of the moment, as I remembered bumblebees swirling noisily around this patio on brighter days. The magic surrounding this place was dying.

I hated to see anything suffering needlessly. "Perhaps I should go outside and put it out of its misery," I said to no one in particular.

But before I could slide open the *mampara,* I heard the call: "Marie, we need your help on the computer."

I pulled myself back to my only assigned task. On the open top-floor landing, next to a large grandfather clock, the computer was perched on the drop-down ledge of the old English secretary, at an angle that made me nervous. Gingerly depressing the keys, I managed to update the large spreadsheet without further damage to the desk.

I finished the updates and handed out copies to the brothers and sisters, who threw dice to determine who would make the first selection. They went around and around, making their selections – throwing dice again for items desired by multiple siblings. Over their heads was an ancient oil painting of the Virgin Mary kneeling and crying at the foot of the cross, arms crossed over her chest. On the ground beside her were symbols of the crucifixion, among them a pair of dice. And so it was again by the throw of dice that possessions were divided among the recipients. Witnessing this as an outsider gave me the chills.

To respect this delicate time, I left the English secretary and made my way through the door leading into Hiltrud's long, narrow sewing room. It was in this room that the youngest generation loved to nap while their grandmother sewed. I could almost hear squeals of delight echoing from the handmade puppet stage that still stood, waiting for the next show. Leaving the sewing room, I turned right toward the upstairs hall and into the bedroom to the right, which was decorated with native motifs and a collection of prints depicting traditions from old Lima. The clicking of the high-voltage security system housed in that room drowned out the voices downstairs. I opened the wooden louvered closet doors and encountered two antique religious statues of Mary and Saint John in Spanish colonial dress. Having seen similar statues in homes of other family members, I knew that they were created to stand at the foot of a cross, which had long since disappeared. *Who will care for these? I thought.* So I took them in my arms, with plans to take them back to our Texas living room, and retraced my steps back to the clock landing.

By the time I returned to the landing, the division was almost complete. I remember Jaime inherited two antique carved front doors from Cuzco and two antique oil paintings of Virgins that hung in the upstairs hallway. Being the only descendent who was a craftsman, Jaime took his father's collection of antique woodworking tools. He also inherited a folding English table with carved heads on its corners previously located in the master suite, various brass pieces from around the fireplace, a branding iron with the intertwined AC letters, a matching pair of small, antique Spanish three-legged milking chairs, some heavily embroidered heirloom table linens, a number of silver serving platters, a hand-turned wood and brass *brasero* (brazier), and two antique Persian rugs the color of dried blood. The most distinctive piece was a large and wonderfully tooled silver frame with the family crest engraved on its raised top. It held an elegant photo of their great-grandfather, Manuel, Ambassador to the U.S. and later to Chile. He looked so distinguished with his ample grey beard and ceremonial uniform adorned with ornate gold braid.

Paco inherited the tall wardrobe-cum-whimsical bar with its elaborate cornice, the rolling bar serving cart from the patio, his grandfather's silver tea set elaborately engraved with the intertwined letters AC, and the painting of Mary at the cross with the dice. Jorge inherited an elaborate *brasero* and various large antique religious oils, including the one in the dining room depicting the Double Trinity with angel musicians at their feet. Teresa took the English secretary, the grandfather clock, and several large antique religious oils. Lichi asked for the wooden stereo cabinet, elaborately carved by her father, some old but valuable decorative apothecary jars, her mother's German Meissen china, and a set of three white egg cups painted with tiny orange flowers. These egg cups were special because each one was a different shade of grey, baked by the intense smoke from the Allied bombing of Darmstadt.

As the day moved into evening, the family maids prepared a very special "last supper" in the dining room. I cannot remember exactly what was served, but the scene is etched in my mind forever. Entertaining guests at home by serving elegant meals is a key part of Lima social and family life. I have many fond memories of such events, which we continue to this day. This last supper was particularly special because the maids had cooked many of Hiltrud's favorite dishes and set the table with the family's most treasured table linens, china, and silver platters. The illuminated patio walls allowed us to look through a *mampara* onto the outside dining area, where I had taken my last siesta. On the adjoining dining room wall we gazed through a large plate glass window with iron lattice work that held pink geraniums in green pots, and onto the lighted *piscinita*. It would be impossible to count the thousands of meals hosted in this room, but we all knew this was truly the last supper we would ever enjoy in this house. The air was filled with elegance and the sense of a Eucharistic feast, as Santa Rosa and the heavenly hosts gazed down on us from the large Double Trinity painting hanging over the sideboard.

The days that followed were relentless. Crews worked both day and night shifts to remove the antique carved doors and replace them with new wooden doors, which they insisted on coating with layer after layer of shiny varnish. My futile attempts to clear the mid-winter air of the suffocating fumes led to a frigid redefinition of the word "open house."

How sad it is to hear people say, "My mother never used her wedding china." Hiltrud didn't believe in that; she shared her beautiful things with the family so we'd remember her love. Looking closely at our inherited treasures, we saw that every piece had some damage. There were dents in the silver, small cracks in the china figurines, little holes in the tablecloths, and slight tears in the elaborately embroidered lace borders. We were fortunate that in Lima there were still crafts people who refurbished "gently used" articles. We took the tablecloths to have the holes rewoven, the lace to be reworked, the silver to have the dents removed and handles soldered, silver plate replated, and even china to be mended. My favorite restoration involved a set of three lovely cream-colored Italian Chinese figures about ten inches tall, in flowing gowns, holding out gifts of water and food. We called them *"Los Chinos Rotos,"* the broken Chinamen, because they were so delicate they had lost hands, feet, and parts of the baskets they were carrying. When we picked up *Los Chinos Rotos* from the restorers, they looked like new. Today they stand proudly on the glass coffee table in the middle of our Texas living room – the same room that the gypsy had described decades before. Whenever I see them, I remember Christ's words, "Behold, I make all things new."

Jaime worked for days in the cold, winter mist constructing a huge crate that would hold the larger of his inherited pieces. He was assisted by José, the loyal gardener, and occasionally by me, as I attempted to dodge the carpenters and varnish fumes. When the crate was finished, we loaded the doors, the English table, the *brasero*, and other heirlooms, and, with the finality reminiscent of sealing a coffin, nailed the crate shut. A truck was hired to carry the box to the airport for air shipment the day after we left.

Jaime and I had been away from work for ten days when it came time to say our goodbyes. Doris (who had named her son Paco, after Jaime's father) was recovering from her C-section earlier that month. Certain that I would never see any of the employees again, I went up to the maid's quarters, teary-eyed, hugged Doris and gave her some extra money. Only God knew what she was going to do after the house was sold. I also said farewell to José the gardener, wondering how he would find work in those terrible economic times.

I went back downstairs to the living room to encounter the family engaged in animated conversations. "Oh God," I cried, tears rolling down my cheeks, holding up my hands in distress, "How can all this *end*?"

I looked around. Was I the only one crying? Was there something that I didn't understand?

Then I looked outside to the patio and witnessed two signs I shall never forget.

"Jaime, there's an off-white squirrel looking straight at us!"

"That can't be a squirrel. There *are no* squirrels in Lima, much less off-white ones." But joining me by the *mampara,* he saw it too. Then I looked down at the patio tiles to see if the maids had swept up the bumblebee, which by then had been dead for well over a week. They had not; the ill-fated bumblebee still lay there on its back. Death and loss was everywhere. But what was that? I rubbed my eyes and got Jaime's attention again.

"Look, do you see that bumblebee moving?" I pointed down to the patio floor.

"No. I don't believe it," he said under his breath.

We looked, then crouched down and looked again. The bumblebee began to stir, and jerked until it flipped over, stretched out its dry wings, and *flew away*.

A year later, we found ourselves again in Lima, at a *Misa del Año,* a special Mass commemorating the lives of Paco and Hiltrud. It was held in La Capillita de La Reparación, a beautiful white stone church down the street from the family's original Avenida Pardo house, and near the Miraflores Park. It was to this small church that Hiltrud went every Sunday morning to hear Father Mauermamo officiating at the 10:30 Mass. This was the only church in Lima where both the mass and the singing were conducted in German, Hiltrud's native tongue. The family remembers Hiltrud kneeling in front of the Virgin in the little chapel on the right, praying that she would have many, very good children. And God granted her wish.

The celebrant at the *Misa del Año* was Bobby Burns, a Jesuit priest and a cousin. The extended "immediate" family of perhaps a hundred people, as well as the employees, filled the little church. We celebrated Paco and Hiltrud, two loving people of great faith, who had undoubtedly lived their lives to the fullest.

Being part of these rites of passage made me feel that I had been fully accepted as a trusted member of Jaime's family. His brothers and sisters allowed me to see them during one of their most vulnerable times. I don't know how many families could turn what so often becomes an occasion for great discord into something more akin to a religious rite of passage. It meant the world to me. Forever after, I knew that whenever I was given the opportunity, I would increasingly share my life with this family. This experience set the stage for everything that was to follow.

Death is not the end of existence; it is only a passing on to a new dimension. Whenever I take the time, I see signs the "departed" send from the other side. I learned that what looked like *the end* was really another *beginning*. What mattered now was that we *acted on* what those on the other side had taught us and what they had left us. I learned that possessions mean nothing unless they carry a message of love. I learned that the liturgies of death, passing, and rebirth need not only happen in a church: that these sacraments are being played out for us every day of our lives – if we only have the eyes to see them.

Our Lady of the Angels, by Ruben Aponte, has provided inspiration during some of our most trying times.

7

A Moveable Store

"No, gracias."

A young Indian woman in a tan conical felt hat holding a drooling serape-swathed baby was peering down into my passenger-side window, trying to sell me small hard candies out of a plastic bag.

"Tres por un sol," she offered, about ten U.S. cents each.

"No, gracias," I shook my head. What more could I say?

Receiving two negative responses and facing a stale red light, the young mother moved on to the next car. She was quickly replaced by an older Indian woman, about four-foot-eight with thin, graying braids, mahogany-tone leathered skin, and a colorful horizontal-striped woolen skirt under which she was partially hiding several petticoats. She assumed her best whining voice and downturned mouth. As she pressed one hand to my window for money, in the other she held a dry rag precariously perched over our windshield, as if threatening to smear the dust. If we paid her off, she might go away.

"¡Ayúdame, Señora!" her well-rehearsed voice pleaded over and over.

"¡NO, GRACIAS!" I shook my head decisively; still she pleaded.

"I keep telling those vendors I don't want what they're offering," I complained to Jaime. "How do I get them to *leave me alone?*"

"Ignore them."

"As a young lady in Texas, when someone offered me something I didn't want *I* was taught to look people in the eye, smile sweetly, nod, and politely say, 'No thank you'."

"If you look at them, they'll think you're interested in what they are selling and they will *never* leave us in peace," Jaime was growing impatient, as the vendors were also beginning to press on the driver's side.

On the streets of Lima the quantity of goods available for purchase from the convenience of your car is astounding. Every day the street vendors seem to come up with a new collection of goods to try the imagination. This method of purchasing is most efficient, since it eliminates the need to look for a parking space and to enter a regular store. It is the epitome of instant gratification and good service. To enhance the experience, the street vendor may even demonstrate the use of their merchandise to anyone who will look. Vendors carry an enormous variety of everything from school and office supplies, electronics accessories, flowers, toys, and fruit. Since traffic causes lengthy delays, vendors carry popular snacks: tubes of nuts, chocolates, and even crisp *barquillos*, those fragile tubular wafer cookies.

On one trip from San Isidro over the hill to La Molina, I saw a little Indian woman demonstrating thigh-toning machines, men selling every type of cell phone cover imaginable, and women presenting plates of perfect pears. On another street corner were men with racks of self-help books, others selling a wide variety of sun glasses. Further down the road were bunny rabbits, windshield wipers, fly swatters, and jump ropes. And there are always the flower vendors, specializing in roses.

Personally, I have bought such diverse items as street maps, DVDs, nail clippers, a magnifying glass, kids' coloring books, sun glasses, cell phone chargers, pencils, pears, roses, and metal rulers. I've even thought about buying the oh-so-necessary plastic mustaches attached to a nose that lights up in a choice of colors: red, orange or purple. I have also bought bananas, which are sold by the "hand," meaning five bananas at a time, and in three popular varieties: *plátano de seda*, which all North Americans recognize as bananas, *plátano de la isla*, a shorter, broader-shaped banana I prefer to eat cooked, as well as tiny three-inch-long "finger" bananas, the delight of small children.

Yet the problem with buying bananas – or any other item – from a street vendor is negotiating a price, paying, and taking possession of the product, all before the light turns green. I remember sitting at one stop light with daughter, Kristy, and her husband, Jason. It was about 8 p.m. and thus well after the normal 6:30 sunset. We were all hungry. Up came a street vendor with just what we needed – bananas! I thrust my hand deep in my purse.

"Darn, I don't have any change."

"Here, I've got some; take mine," Jason was quick to volunteer.

I held my hand out towards the back seat and Jason filled it with coins.

"Wow, what a lot of small change!" I thought. Sure that Jason had counted it first, I thrust the entire amount into the vendor's hand.

"OK?" I asked him, as he handed over his entire stock, five *hands* of bananas, in return.

The vendor paused, and then a broad smile crossed his face, for he had received this surprise windfall at the most fortuitous moment – just as the light turned green. As Jaime slowly drove off, the vendor looked me straight in the eye, nodded, crossed himself, and bowed.

"How much change did you *give* me?" I asked Jason.

"I don't know. It was everything I *had*."

Oops. This was for sure the banana vendor's luckiest day ever. I had probably handed him several days' earnings.

On yet another drive...

"EEEEkkk. What was *that?*" I threw my hands up and screamed as a vendor pressed an eight-inch hairy grey rat with a long pink tail against my window. Looking again, I noticed with great relief, "Oh, its fake! How *crass*. What kind of sick-o would buy a fake rat?" I complained. Then I reconsidered, "Hey! That could be a *great* gag gift." I knew *just* the friend who warned us she might not return for another weekend of hospitality at our beach house because she was afraid we might have mice. Jaime nixed the idea of the fake rat. OK, I had to agree that it *did* redefine the word *tasteless*, not to mention that Jaime has never been a fan of shopping from a car.

Street vendors often tailor their wares to both season and occasion, so closely that they seem to be supplied by some unseen street vendor coalition. I ticked off the holidays...

Valentine's Day? Roses.

Easter? Bunnies and plastic eggs.

Back to school? Binders and pencils.

Halloween? Costumes, some even mimicking popular political characters.

On New Year's Eve, all the street vendors in Lima are outfitted with firecrackers, which are bought by the tens of thousands from the convenience of cars. That the city has an ordinance prohibiting the use of explosives is beside the point. Once a motorist has acquired these "weapons of mass destruction," what is to keep him from shooting off a few? The suffocating, two-story-high smoke that greets the New Year is testimony to the winner in this game. Chalk one up for the street vendors.

In Lima, however, street life consists of more than vendors. Should you miss your theater appointment because of traffic, never worry: there is entertainment just around the corner. Lima is full of street kids who have learned to survive by entertaining drivers. On the most frequented street corners there are groups of these enterprising children performing everything from juggling, rudimentary gymnastics and break dancing, to musical shows. At night, if you are lucky, you may get to see a fire eater. They live on tips – one sol (30 cents) will do.

Since the mid-80s the streets of Lima have been virtually invaded by minibuses, called *combis* or *micros*. They are a blessing to the working class and the bane of everyone with a car. *Micros* are almost always white, with assorted colorful stripes. Some of them are labeled with Asian letters, perhaps castoffs from Japan. Others find humor in advertising features that no *micro* has ever had. We saw one the other day that had given itself a five-star rating, sporting icons for air conditioning, TV, food, reclining seats, and bathrooms!

As of this writing, nearly one hundred percent of the *micros* belch black soot into Lima's already contaminated environment. *Micros*, and really all forms of public transportation, are so packed during the morning and afternoon rush periods that there is standing room only. Jaime's brother Jorge rides a *micro* to and from work each day. He tells stories of poor people, crazy people, con artists, beggars, and thieves. For some reason, he feels that he is beyond danger. Or perhaps he feels the entertainment is worth the risk.

"Of course they won't rob me. I ride the bus to work every day," he assured us.

The most interesting part of all of this is that Jorge will not, regardless of the amount of persuasion, take a taxi. "Too expensive," he always says, even though he is one of the top managers of a textile factory.

"I don't feel like getting into all that traffic to go out to eat," I griped one evening.

"Let's order in," Jaime volunteered.

Delivery services take on a new meaning in Lima, where almost anything that one might buy in a store can be brought to a house via *pedido,* ordering out. *Pedidos* are most frequently delivered by motorcycles, which find it easier to navigate Lima's congested streets. To identify as well as advertise the company, on the motorcycle seat sits a large plastic representation of the service being delivered. For instance, a drugstore delivering prescriptions uses a white plastic doctor with a stethoscope, smiling and facing backwards. As in all countries, pizza and Chinese food can be delivered, but roast chicken delivery is also quite popular. A Lima icon, Pardo's Chicken, keeps your food hot in a discrete white box with their name, while competitor Mediterranean Chicken hopes to gain sales by bringing a large plastic yellow chicken along for the ride. Playa Asia, a popular summer getaway, has every delivery service imaginable, including a Sushi Pronto years before they even *sold* sushi in Texas. Wong, Peru's largest grocery store chain, of course delivers. So does Santa, a small fresh produce shop owner in Chacarilla — but her delivery vehicle is a bicycle.

Recently Jaime and I were driving behind a *McDonald's* delivery motorcycle! Really, this was going *way* too far.

Don't want to take your dog out for his weekly washing? No problem, animal cleaning services come to your residence in a white van to pick up and drop off your pet. Need your knives sharpened? Just listen for the friendly TWEE-dle whistle of the guy with the big metal wheel. Like freshly baked bread? Look for the bicycle with the big white box over the front wheel. Ice cream in the summer – or winter? Hail one of the competitive D'Onofrio and Lamborgini guys on their bicycles.

When we were ill, we were grateful that our family doctor made house calls. The local laboratory sent a neatly-uniformed young lady to do in-house lab tests, the results of which we accessed that afternoon *online*. In Lima we don't have any "privacy law" problems in getting our own test results – like we have in the U.S.!

Growing up in Texas, I knew for sure that a *store* had a fixed location, a license, and sign in front with its name. This isn't true in Peru, where anyone with a rag and a bucket or a bag of candy can start a little business. People there do not wait in an unemployment line for their next job; direct services can be sold to any available customer. This mentality has come in particularly handy during times of unstable economies and high unemployment.

At first glance, it came as quite a surprise to learn that a developing country could have so many services. But the longer I am in Peru, the more I realize that services like these are one of the many symbiotic ways that the rich and poor are able to live peacefully in close proximity. Without this interchange, the lifestyles of both would be endangered.

Myself, I have gone from disdaining street vendors and the ever-present delivery motorcycles to enjoying the view, always looking for a new twist. The latest was a literal *fleet* of Pardo's Chicken delivery motorcycles, all lined up along a popular road, holding their breath in expectation as the Saturday evening orders poured in. Come to think of it, I could use some of that chicken about right now.

What we saw that day was a desert beach, but not far in
the future there would be houses with so much glass
that parts of them seemed transparent.

8

A Glimpse of Heaven

The first day we were in Lima on this particular visit, Tere, the younger of Jaime's two sisters, called. "I'm coming by tomorrow morning to pick you up. I've just bought a lot in the new Brisas beach development. It's in Playa Asia."

"Why would Tere want a beach lot?" I asked Jaime. "Their home has a large yard, a private park in back, and they have a membership at the Club Villa. Besides, why is Playa Asia so great?"

"Playa Asia is a long beach about an hour to the south. People say it will become the next Ancón." replied Jaime. I remembered from many family stories that Ancón had been *the* beach to be seen at in the 1960s – the pre-terrorist era. I was looking forward to a very interesting trip.

The next morning Teresa wheeled up in her gold Peugeot SUV, her short blonde hair blowing in the breeze, singing along with music from an aria of the opera Rigoletto, in full surround sound. It took over an hour to get to Playa Asia. From the *Panamericana*, there was no sign that we were entering a developed area. All we could see for miles around were sand dunes. We turned right onto a rocky unpaved road. A mile down, we cleared a checkpoint with uniformed armed guards, then turned right again, through a guard station and into what looked exactly like a fenced-in desert. Tere drove around a circular dirt and gravel road, bringing her SUV to a screeching stop on a bare beach. She jumped out of the car and waved her hands at the smooth tan sand saying, "What do you think of my lot?"

"*This* is where you are going to build a beach house?" I said in disbelief. "There is absolutely *nothing* here!"

"Ah, but there will be," replied Tere, her blue eyes flashing. "There will be."

Since the Las Palmas, Cayma, and Los Cocos communities already existed at Playa Asia, it took just a few years for the Brisas development to take off. After the first row of houses was completed, a second row of houses were built, then a third. Tennis courts and grassy children's playgrounds sprang up, then a clubhouse. Irrigation turned the desert scape into lush gardens. With every summer, the transformation was beyond belief. Tere's family had constructed a lovely one-story, five-bedroom, five-bath house, complete with a long open hallway filled with climbing bougainvilleas, a swimming pool, covered porch, and a coffee table with a marble dolphin jumping through its glass top. By then her desert lot had tripled in value.

Shortly afterward, Paco and Ana Teresa bought a lot behind Tere's. The crazy idea of having a beach house was infectious, but the area was remote. Groceries had to be carried by car from Lima or bought in neighboring open-air markets in the not-so-near towns of Cañete or Mala. But it did not matter, the developments along Playa Asia kept multiplying and the families kept coming. The attraction of the beach was as compelling to Peruvians as it was to the Franklin Gulls that migrated there from the plains of North America.

Why are Peruvians so attracted to the beach? As every North American knows, equatorial beaches can do a tremendous amount of damage to human skin, hair, and eyes. Besides, how could anyone, much less those "poor" Peruvians, afford even the sand to sit on to watch the waves of the Pacific collide with the shore?

It seems to me that in the U.S. many people are absorbed with job security, planning for retirement, and investments. South Americans understand that the veneer of civilization is very thin, that politics and economics are unpredictable, and that the only things that count are the closeness of generations and sharing the beauty of each day.

While many Peruvians may not be "rich" by North American standards, a surprising number own beach homes. Acquiring a beach lot and constructing a suitable place to house a family and a few friends (4-6 bedrooms, sleeping 8-18 people), along with a separate bedroom and bath for the maids, can be more a matter of priorities than of extra cash on hand. In a land where families and friends are the priority and are often numerous, a beach house in a gated community is the summer haven for young children to play in safety and peace, where adolescents can meet and date, and where grown children can return with their own families to enjoy the summer months of December through March.

These years, the most popular Peruvian beaches are located south of Lima off the *Panamericana*. The beaches all have names, but there are so many of them along the cove-lined Pacific Coast that their precise address is often identified by kilometer location. Unless someone knows the kilometer location of a particular beach, it is unlikely that they will be able to find it in a day. The beach where Teresa literally put her stake in the sand is located at kilometer 98, approximately 59 miles south of Lima. Entrance gates are staffed by guards with walkie-talkies. Any non-resident who wishes to visit a beach development must show a legal ID, a house number and owner's name, and their hosts must call the gate in advance.

Travel time to and from Lima depends entirely on the time of day. On particularly busy days it can take as long to get outside Lima's city limits as it does to complete the rest of the trip. Since weekend trips to the beach are such a priority, the government has minimized the traffic jam by turning all but one lane of the divided *Panamericana* into a one-way highway during certain hours. Since everyone *knows* that no sane person would go to the beach on Sunday afternoon or return to Lima on Saturday morning, three of the four lanes become one-way during those times. Pity the tourist who arrives in Lima on Sunday afternoon and decides to take a drive south!

Before I must return to my windowless office in a Texas chemical manufacturing complex, let me record how it feels to be truly *alive*.

I am sitting in the living room of Paco and Ana Teresa's beach house, looking through a wall of glass, and past a covered patio, at a flawless day. There is not a cloud in the crystal blue sky. The air is dry and remarkably cool, due to the Humboldt Current that runs along the western side of South America. No matter how hot the sun is, and the equatorial sun can be cruel, any spot of shade offers a gentle repose.

Today the ocean is Copen blue and calm, with a single row of glistening white waves. The shore is dotted with a neat line of brightly colored *sombrillas* (beach umbrellas) in tomato red, traffic yellow, emerald green, and royal blue, next to elegant cotton tents in the purest white. These are set up and taken down each day by a small army of beach employees, who also rake the sand each morning to remove any trace of debris before the homeowners descend for their daily tan. During the day, a stream of friendly local vendors provide a wide variety of refreshments, ice creams, hats, bags, and jewelry, all of which can be charged directly to a house number.

All the houses in this development have flat roofs and are made of reinforced concrete and brick, covered with a thin layer of finishing cement and painted an almost blinding white. Wooden window shutters on the bedrooms are finished with natural stains, or painted dark teal, canary yellow, or royal blue. Tall, often frameless, sliding glass *mamparas* face the ocean. Some of the houses have so much glass that they appear to be completely transparent. To add to the transparency, the second floors of some houses contain swimming pools with a glass wall. Remembering the saying about people who live in glass houses, I surmise that no one at this beach throws stones.

Occasionally an interior wall is painted terra-cotta, evoking the original Indian inhabitants who used the same color to honor the setting sun. The walls and ceilings are dotted with strategically-placed glass bricks and skylights. To add even more light, floors are often made of large white Italian tiles which flow seamlessly from room to room, and onto roofless hallways and covered terraces. Flowerbeds and potted plants provide bursts of brilliant colors and swimming pools reflect the cloudless sky.

Along the white walls run an array of lush flowering tropical plants. The most prominent are a profusion of blood red, magenta, orange, peach, and fuchsia bougainvilleas climbing the walls and spilling over patios and doorways. Below the climbing plants are hedges of yellow and red hibiscus, and below them, rows of geraniums in brilliant colors, ranging from light pink to glowing red to burgundy. Artfully sculpted flowerbeds are filled with more flowering plants and a wide variety of flowering cactus, and are bounded by flagstones dotting the grassy lawns. The beauty of this scene is all the more rare, since this profusion of botanical life exists in the middle of a desert.

The desert? I almost forgot to mention it, because when facing the ocean it does not seem to exist. However, an about-face reveals that within a half mile of the beach and behind several rows of houses, civilization appears to end. Easily visible from the back of the houses are five to seven layers of foothills, which continue beyond my sight, endlessly rolling upward until they become the mighty Andes. The hills are absolutely bare of vegetation, as it never really rains along this coast. Yet even devoid of vegetation, these desert hills are filled with colors. The first layer is golden with delicate black streaks, the second light grey, and the next tan, depending on the trace mineral content. Hills with copper deposits appear green. The layers continue soaring upwards in shades of hunter green, burgundy, midnight blue, and deepest purple until they meet the clouds.

Back in the beach house, the gentle ocean breeze provides a constant stream of the purest air. Somewhere, I can hear a wind chime gently toning in the breeze. The stereo fills the room with the music of Julio Iglesias and Antonio Carlos Jobin. Veronica, the maid, has just finished cleaning the house and is beginning to prepare lunch. Today lunch consists of *corvina* (the famous South American sea bass), locally-grown asparagus, and tree-ripened mangos. The delicate odor of sautéed garlic drifts through the air. Large tree-ripened avocados and sweet tomatoes are mixed into the salad. Peruvian garlic rice, puree of uniquely-Peruvian yellow potatoes, boiled *choclo* (Peru's white horse-tooth corn), and baked naturally candy-sweet *camote* (Peruvian sweet potatoes) are also on the menu. For dessert there is a chilled torte made of the thinnest layers of meringue, interlaced with fudge and *lúcuma* cream. How so many Latin women maintain their youthful figures in the presence of such food continues to be a mystery to me.

What is there "to do" at the beach? Actually, quite a number of things, beginning with getting up late, eating, drinking, swimming, surfing and tanning all day, and attending parties in the evenings that, if you are young enough, can last until after sunrise. Other than this typical routine, there are several sacred beach rituals. Surely these rituals began with the earliest Indian inhabitants, because they provide a timeless regeneration of the body and the spirit.

A ritual practiced by all inhabitants is eating, which occurs throughout the day, with meals at generally accepted intervals. A continental breakfast can be taken any time between 7 and 10 a.m. Snacks, including alcoholic beverages, begin around noon, usually down at the beach. Lunch is served as the sun begins to wane, around 3 but sometimes as late as 4 or 5 p.m. Dinner is served at or after 9:30, which is either excellent for the parties that kick off around midnight or can lead to some interesting dreams for those who choose to retire "early."

Tanning is another ritual, the one for which I am least prepared, since I have just come from North America and it is February. No red-blooded Latin is without a healthy tan and no young Latin can imagine that there may be skin cancer, cataracts, wrinkles, or sunspots looming in their future. From the looks of older Latins, I am not at all sure that these infirmities afflict them at the same rate they do their northern neighbors. Tans range from golden brown to mahogany, making it difficult to believe that the skin underneath is often quite white. Since it is not possible to get a good tan in just a few days, this is a ritual in which I participate minimally. Today, I am feeling the effects of too much participation yesterday.

The most universally-popular activity is a morning or evening stroll along the shore, or a bicycle ride along the tiled walkways that connect the houses to the parks. In the mornings, this activity often coincides with the daily migration of wildlife from one end of the beach to the other. There is so much wildlife here that I am certain that under some beach front patio sits a wildlife photographer, working under the extreme conditions of a cold Cusqueña beer and maid service, to capture the "wild" beauty of the Peruvian coastline.

A morning walk disturbs flocks of resting sea birds, including large black and white Kelp Gulls, fussy Grey Gulls, black and white Skimmers with their red feet and beaks, and Grey Pelicans flying in formation. The local bird population uses several uninhabited rock islands offshore as nesting sites. The ocean is populated with huge schools of cold-water fish, families of large dolphins, several large seals and an occasional sea otter, all of whom delight in evading swimmers braving the 60 degree Fahrenheit waters. A walk at dusk takes us past houses where opera music drifts through the cool evening breeze. The translucent waves bear cadres of young men preparing to ride the day's last wave. The figures of animals and humans alike turn ebony against the sun's last golden glow.

My favorite ritual, and the only one that occurs in a predictable timeframe, is saluting the setting sun, *la puesta del sol*. This ritual is most properly performed from the patio of a beach house with a good view of the ocean, and with a *pisco sour* or other appropriate drink in hand. A good sunset can be so striking that even the most expressive Latin has been known to face the ocean in awe and momentarily cease all communication. For those who have not had the privilege, let me describe the daily cycle – for all sunsets must first begin with a sunrise.

To me, the entire scenario is the interplay between two great forces: sun and ocean. The sun is the masculine force, represented in sound by the "OMmm" that so many cultures recognize during times of meditation. The ocean is the feminine force, represented by the undulating "ah-AH-ah" sound attributed to the sirens that were said to drive sailors into rocky coasts. Traversing these two great forces by diving straight into the ocean in search of food are pure white birds called Peruvian Boobies, with their high-pitched cries.

Each day the sun begins its cycle, rising shortly after 6 a.m. from behind the Andean foothills. During the night, the ocean has done her work, covering the ground with a fine haze. The sun rises quickly and begins its task of drying up the haze. Throughout the day, it is unrelenting, scorching everything in its path.

Shortly after noon, the over-confident sun decides to take on the ocean, an unwise move indeed. The closer the sun moves towards that undulating siren, the more its power diminishes. A half hour before sunset, the sun is a huge glowing orb hanging over the water. The offshore islands first turn gold and then black, and the water becomes a pool of liquid gold. Dolphins and seals gather to frolic in the luxurious light.

As the day ends, the water forms clouds, filtering out the sun's last rays into an array of glowing colors: rose, Italian blue, and the striking terra-cotta. It is at this moment that the ocean accepts the sun into its depths and the two become one.

The sunset is the union of these two eternal forces, the sun and the ocean, and the salute from the beach house patio a just recognition of the interplay of nature's divine elements. It is with this ritual that a perfect day finds its end.

What living being, after experiencing time at this beach, could possibly resist making sacrifices to return here every summer? For those who have never been here, coming may be a matter of priorities. But for those of us who have lived the experience, being here is an expression of life itself.

Over the years I have come to understand that the beach experience is not only about the sun and the ocean. It is about finding a large, clean, private place where people can share their common heritage and safely enjoy nature at its best. Here the residents have gone through a selection process and many even have common ancestors. Parents can leave their children in private parks with their nannies, then later go to a dinner or a dance, walk home along the beach, then sit outside on their patios with their family and friends, until late at night.

The more I understood about Peruvian family values, the more having a beach house made sense. I especially remember the nights, under starry skies and a full moon, talking with the family and singing ballads in Spanish. This was nothing like my experiences at beach houses along the Texas coast. This was family bonding at its best.

Each summer, I found myself crying – sobbing openly at the thought of returning to the daily grind in the U.S. How would I resolve this tearing at my heart? Only time would tell.

Part II

A Stake in the Sand

1997 – 2006

On our first visit to Conchitas beach, February 1997, dolphins
were riding the waves, jumping backwards in unison. It looked
like something out of SeaWorld.
L-R: Paco, Lichi, Jorge, Tere, and Jaime.

9

Our Slice of Paradise

It is just past lunchtime, about 4:00 p.m. on a sunny March day. The remains of a sumptuous lunch of Mediterranean-style salad, *papas rellenas* (mashed potatoes stuffed with herb-filled meat) and *salsa de rocoto* (red-hot chili sauce), followed by a dessert of the sweetest *melon* (cantaloupe), *chirimoya*, orange pound cake and espresso is settling happily in my stomach. The rest of the family has retired for a nap, but the *rocoto* sauce is helping me to stay awake to record some memories of the incredible past three years.

They say to be careful of what you wish for, because some dreams, no matter how impossible, can come true. Well, for us they did.

This chapter of our lives began on February 5, 1997. The Infinite manifested itself in the form of an invitation from Jaime's brothers and sisters to travel southward to visit a new beach development called Conchitas. We had heard about this beach earlier, as a few members of Jaime's extended family had lots there. The route was, of course, via the *Panamerica*, the intercontinental highway along which run, like a string of pearls, the beach resorts that dot the coastline south of Lima.

The beach we were to visit was completely different than Playa Asia, where we had been hosted for several years by members of Jaime's family. While Playa Asia was totally flat, with most hills in the distant background, at Conchitas the hills descended sharply to the ocean. This phenomenon was not immediately apparent as we passed through the gate in the bamboo security wall of the compound. All we could see were huge dunes and cliffs with the tourmaline-blue sea appearing now and then over the tops of the golden dunes. Driving downhill from the gate, we encountered a sharp T-intersection, with a view that made each of us catch our breath. Just past the sidewalk that ran atop the ridge was a perilous drop of over 100 feet that ended in a magnificent, uninhabited horseshoe beach. On either side of the beach, rocky hills and tall boulders met the ocean. On the left-hand side lay two other, smaller beaches, consisting almost entirely of rocks, but equally as lovely and even more secluded.

We parked the car atop a hill on the far left-hand side of the beach, at the spot where Jaime's two cousins planned to build their mirror-image houses. The heat of the day was intense and the sun was blinding. As beautiful as this place was, I was ready to go back to Playa Asia and have a cold drink. But Jaime's brothers and sisters would hear nothing of it. Clothes came off revealing bathing suits beneath. Together, they ran straight down the hill and towards the water. The abandon that they exhibited in a deserted beach worried me.

I felt alone and exposed to danger in this uninhabited area, my thoughts going wild. *What if there is an undertow? What if the water is too cold? Unfriendly sea life could be lurking beneath the surface! There are no doctors nearby.*

No one was listening to my warnings, nor were they inclined to wait for me, so I bit my lip and slid down the hill after them, grumbling all the way. Stripping down to my bathing suit, I nudged myself toward the ocean. Everyone else was already in the water, so I *had* to follow or be left behind. Yes, the water was cold, about 60 degrees Fahrenheit. There were a few dead fish lying around. Swimming half-way towards Jaime, I saw him being lured toward some type of a sinkhole in the middle of the lagoon just off this tiny beach. Hoping against despair that some answer would come I cried inside, *Dear God, where are you?* Before I could get to him, Jaime popped free and swam back towards me. The others were getting out of the water and drying off. It all happened so fast.

We climbed back up the high hill and took photos of ourselves and of the five brothers and sisters, their backs to the ocean and the coastline. Until that moment, I felt no special connection to this beach. Then, as we turned to leave, something happened which we shall never forget. While standing on the cliff, we turned our heads towards the main beach area and saw dolphins "surfing" the translucent green waves. We watched in amazement for some time. Then three dolphins rode a wave together and, as the wave neared the shore, they simultaneously jumped completely clear of the water and landed on the back side of the wave. It was a scene directly out of SeaWorld, yet there was no trainer. Jaime and I stared at each other and we each inhaled deeply and held our breath. After watching the dolphins jump repeatedly over a period of time, we realized that this was no mirage.

Thomas Keating summarized our feelings so well when he said, "Every now and then God lifts a corner of the veil and enters into our awareness through various channels, as if to say, 'Here I am. Where are you? Come and join me'."

Since we were already there at the beach and didn't know when, or if, we would return, we thought it not a bad idea to take a look at how the lots were divided. We walked around from lot to lot, judging the views. The lots were so small that it seemed impossible to build a house on them, but then I remembered that in most Latin American houses, living occurs on patios within walls and not in the yard outside.

We selected a couple of favorite views and casually inquired about the prices, which seemed incredibly high, considering the size of the lots.

We considered the views and took more photos. When we returned to Lima, we got a call saying that the prices of the lots were going up.

"So what's it to us?" Jaime and I shrugged it off.

Our vacation over, we returned to Texas, but try as we might, we could not get the memory of that beach and the dolphins off our mind. We e-mailed Jaime's brother Jorge, with a request to inquire about the lot availability.

"This could make a good investment," said Jaime. "We could buy now and sell if we needed to." A prudent decision for sure.

A couple of months later, after the disappearance and merciful reappearance of a large block of money transferred from the U.S. to a Peruvian bank, we became the proud "investors" in lot 27H at Conchitas beach. Even the number was lucky, as my luck runs in groups of three. Our lot number was 27, or (3 x 3) x 3, commemorating the exact number of years since I had fled Guadalajara.

"So, I wonder what it would cost to build a little house on this little lot... Just a fantasy," I mentioned to Jaime.

Coming back to Texas reality, I worked during the day and at night paced the floors and drew up floor plans. After all, I had taken architectural design and drafting courses in college. "Might as well put that training to some use," I reasoned. I still have my "best" design stashed away in my old Franklin Planner; the design as outdated as the planner itself. I keep it as a memory of the difference in a practical and an inspired design.

We learned about this inspiration when, around Easter of 1997, we asked architect Emilo Soyer to provide us with a "little sketch" of what a little house might look like on our little lot. Time passed and passed.

"It sure is a good thing that we aren't serious about all of this," reasoned Jaime.

With all the wisdom of a virgin on her first date with a playboy, I replied, "Yeah, this whole thing is just a game."

Months later first sketches arrived – who can rush genius? The "little sketch" appeared as a series of electronic three-dimensional drawings, complete with shadows and shrubs. This was no little house. It had four bedrooms and baths plus a maid's bedroom and bath. Instead of a single house, there were two separate buildings. The main house contained the living room, dining room, kitchen, and maid's quarters on the lower floor, with a large master suite above. The guest house contained a bedroom and bath combo downstairs, and a two-bedroom and bath "apartment" upstairs. The two buildings were connected by an open-air staircase, complete with a second-floor bridge to the master suite. The central patio contained a lovely piano-shaped pool with an infinity edge that made the water on the "keyboard" appear to drain into the Pacific. The patio also featured a covered terrace, where we could enjoy lunch. Years later, I would write this memoir from that very terrace.

First drafts are rarely final drafts, and so it was with the house plans. Another bathroom was added for visiting guests.

"What kind of *idiots* would want a beach house in the desert with *five* bathrooms?" we asked ourselves. "Oh ... us."

We modified the plans to carve out more storage space, which would be needed during our long absences. After reading the Conchitas housing regulations, we found that parts of the house had to be redesigned. The redesign took months longer.

As architectural designs are not technical drawings, and our curiosity about the cost of this fantasy house was mounting, we decided to commission a complete set of technical drawings. These drawings cost thousands of dollars and took even more months, being done by respected design engineers, some of whom taught at universities in Lima. As the Peruvian Coast is a seismic area and this house would be built on a cliff of sand and rocks, the foundation included a massive underground system of 30 T-bottomed columns and an underground retaining wall, particularly in the area of the pool, which was on a hill that dropped steeply to the road below then wound its way down to the beach. Using the normal South American reinforced concrete and brick construction, this "house" would be built like a fortress, with sliding glass walls and expanses of windows facing the ocean.

On our next trip to Lima, we sent the drawings out for bids, only to learn that the house would cost *twice* what we anticipated. By the time the bids were returned, it was time to return to Texas. We were utterly exhausted and emotionally drained. There seemed no place to turn. Then we remembered that our future next-door neighbor had recommended we try a new firm made up of a civil engineer and an architect who had just moved to Lima from Ica, a city many hours to the south.

The day we were to leave for Texas, we went to the engineer and architect's office on the walk-up third floor of a working-class office building in Lima's San Borja district. They were just setting up the office. There were cables strung all over, as the phone and computers were not yet connected.

I looked into the eyes of the partners, Hugo and Muriel, and in my most sincere broken Spanish told them, "We have no more time left, our options are used up. We are *very serious* about needing to have your bid be the lowest one."

Hugo explained, "Everyone in our profession has studied the same curriculum. But some of us live more prudently than others." He assured us that they were "very honest Evangelicals," which came as a surprise to us because in those days, almost all Peruvians were Catholics.

Hugo and Muriel told us of renovation projects they were involved with, but reflecting back on it later, we did not ask if they had built a complete house yet. Much later, we were to find out that they hadn't.

Back in Texas, Jaime and I worried and prayed.

"Are we ready to trust our future housing to this pair?" Jaime asked.

"They seem nice and very honest to me. What are our other choices?" I asked.

"Do we have any?"

Within two weeks we received a Fax with a detailed listing of the cost of the house. The price was still 40 percent more than we had planned, but was finally within discussion range. The way that Hugo and Muriel had brought down the price was ingenious. The low-salt sand, an absolute necessity for construction, would come from the south, towards Ica, instead of the north, towards Lima, and would thus cost less. They would not charge us for site visits, but would manage the construction on their way to and from a project in Ica.

We almost cried for joy – we had found our builders!

"But does that mean that we're actually going to build? What happened to this being just a fantasy?" Without realizing it, we had sold ourselves on the insane idea of building a beach house on a sand hill in the earthquake-prone Peruvian coast.

Construction on the house began in early December. This was unusual timing, as most beach house construction starts in late April and must stop between mid-December and mid-April to allow the residents to enjoy the summer. But this beach was so new that there were few residents to bother. Making summer construction more arduous was the advent of El Niño, the warm-water current that disturbs marine life and the weather in general throughout the western hemisphere. The dedicated building supervisor, Maestro Crisóstomo, and his team worked for over five months on the *foundation* alone.

"Remember to be there for the pouring of the slab," our friends in the U.S. advised.

We couldn't seem to get the point across that there was really no "slab," as understood in U.S. terms. That five-months of work *was* the foundation. During that time, the team essentially built an entire house of foundation beneath our house, complete with cistern and swimming pool foundation. Then they filled all of it back in, except for the cistern and pool.

We tell everyone that we built our beach house over the Internet. In essence, this is true, because we were only in Peru for one brief visit during the nine months of construction. In the meantime, Hugo e-mailed us digital photos of the progress. We'll always remember our anxiety and anticipation, sitting at the computer, wine glasses in hand, waiting for those photos to download.

We returned to Peru for a two-week visit during the construction. That trip we picked out tiles, appliances, paint color (white), doorknobs, kitchen cabinets, window styles and sliding glass walls. Our heads were dizzy, juggling costs, durability and colors. Visiting the site, we walked up precariously placed planks to reach our second-floor master bedroom — only to witness a wall being erected where, according to the plans, it should not have been.

"I think I'm going to have a breakdown," I moaned to Jaime.

"This is supposed to be a *window*," Jaime said, as he showed the workers the plans, asking them to remove the bricks. Today that window provides a lovely view of the beach from our bedroom.

The construction area was beyond dirty. The first floor, some day to be accessed from an open-air stairway, was instead reached by a slippery slide down a muddy incline. On the main level, the kitchen looked like a dungeon, long and narrow, full of bare bricks and dirt. Workers were crawling all over the site like an army of ants. Every bit of concrete in our brick, concrete, and rebar house was mixed in a small electric mixer. There were no machines to pour the concrete. Instead, the workers poured each of the five layers of roof by walking up wooden boards, carrying heavy buckets of concrete on their shoulders. Roof pourings using this method are so arduous that there is a tradition that the builder provides dinner and drinks after each one.

As if all of that weren't enough for a two-week "vacation," Jaime's cousin Gloria had obtained a number of Republican-era doors from the demolition of a portion of the house of Pedro Beltrán, a historic figure of Peruvian diplomacy.

"Come over to our storage area and take a look," she said.

"That's just what we need, another project! Why would we want old doors?" I groused.

The door finishes were worn through, but the doors themselves were strong and the designs were beautiful. In back of us stood Mario, the lead carpenter who worked for our builders, silently eyeing the doors. We added up the costs and were utterly surprised with the results.

"Can you believe that these solid wood antique doors and their refinishing will cost us *less* than new hollow-core doors?" Jaime exclaimed.

We didn't know it at the time, but Mario would live on site five days a week, dedicating months of his life to refinishing those 33 doors and fitting them to the door facings. The door project would have to take place while we were in the U.S. It was time to head back to work again.

By late June the beach house was ready for the official sign-off. It was time to head back down to Peru. On July 4, 1998, Jaime, his brother Jorge, and I met with Hugo and Muriel at the beach house. It was mid-winter in Peru; cloudy and terribly depressing. The house was wonderfully built, but still unfurnished. There were walls of bare glass, but no shades. We were running out of funds and were utterly opposed to getting a loan, if such a thing were even available to expats in Lima.

"Have we done the right thing?" Jaime and I asked each other over and over.

"Dear God, I need a sign. Any sign. Just a *sign* that we're doing the right thing," I prayed all day long. "What have we gotten ourselves into?"

The day dragged on. Yard men brought loads of potting soil to fill in all the flowerbeds and yard. A misty drizzle fell all day, making a slippery, muddy mess on the new white flagstone stairs and terracotta-colored tiles. Sweeping and mopping consumed the entire day.

"A sign, please, please God, a sign." I begged, "Just a *little* sign." But it was drawing night and we had no electricity.

"Come on, Marie, we've got to get back to Lima," Jaime said, walking up the stairs to the car. Dejected, I turned my back to the beach and headed towards the stairs.

Just at that moment, Jorge yelled, "Look at the *ocean!*"

I whirled around. The *entire ocean,* as far as we could see, both to the north and to the south, was lit up in undulating waves of neon-green light so bright that, if you were in a boat, you could read a newspaper by it. I could only stand there and cry aloud, "Oh, dear God. Forgive my lack of faith." The spontaneous plankton bloom that caused the ocean to light up that night continued for a full *five months*. It was a very rare event, which to this day – so many years later – has not been repeated. Technically, this was a natural event, but it was the timing that made it an answer to my prayers.

The next three months of work in Texas, waiting for our return to Peru, were excruciatingly long. But the time eventually passed. During our next two-week trip to Peru in October, we ordered hand-made furniture for the house, choosing dark-stained Peruvian cedar to go with the colonial doors.

Returning to the U.S., we worked long distance with craftsmen and Margarita, the family seamstress. We flew to Peru again in January for our first summer at the beach house. Guests poured in. The house I had envisioned as a potential retreat location turned out to be what all Limeños knew it was – a party home. In the years that followed, the beach house has hosted friends and family and has, on some occasions, even managed to provide me with a bit of personal time.

Over the years, the beach has developed some handy services. Despite its remote location, the Conchitas employees will deliver the El Comercio newspaper any day we want it. They will also gladly pick up groceries and other things that we may be missing when they go home to their villages in the evenings. Rosa sells ice cream and drinks down at the beach to eager children – and adults. All of the services are billed to each house and paid every Monday or two.

When we don't want to carry our cooler all the way out to our *sombrilla*, beach employees are waiting, ready to help in their matching white uniforms. Drowning? The yellow-and-red clad life guards are always on the lookout. Hungry? Señora Maria or one of her extensive clan can be contacted via cell phone to pull a tasty fish out of the ocean, bring it still flipping to your door, and filet it in your kitchen – all for less than the same fish would cost in a Lima grocery store. With the help of our dear maid, Doris, we now have our very own slice of paradise.

Then, and now, I believe that we were led to build the beach house. It was no accident at all. This house has changed our perspective of where we call "home" and what we value. It has given us the most precious gifts life can offer: time to be with those we love, and to enjoy God's bounty and the life we've been given.

A shoreline view of the beach house.

All Wet

Ruth Stanford Peale, wife of the dynamic minister and author of "The Power of Positive Thinking," Norman Vincent Peale, always advised her readers: "Find a hole and fill it." For many years, the only hole I found to fill in Lima was at the bottom of a washing machine – and it was someone else's washing machine!

Before I begin my tale of woe, let me first be clear: Peruvians are very concerned with cleanliness, but they go about being clean in an entirely different way than we do in the U.S. People of a certain strata leave domestic duties to maids, who do everything on their own timetable. The normal Peruvian method of sun and wind drying, followed by ironing, works well in the spring and summer – for small amounts of laundry. But this does not work at all during the misty winter or at the end of summer, when the amount of dirty blankets, bedspreads, sheets, and towels are enough to fill a small car.

Our annoying laundry problems stemmed from several deviations from the Peruvian norm. First, we had no washer or dryer at the beach house. Then, we had no place or time to do our last load of summer laundry in Lima, as we stayed at the beach house until the day we were to catch the plane back to the U.S. Unless they have experienced it, no one can imagine how frustrating it is to close up a house recently occupied by ten people, drive one-and-a-half hours to Lima, try to wash a carload full of dirty clothes, sheets, blankets and spreads, complete the job *without* a dryer, and then return to the U.S. that *very night*. It is physically impossible.

There were other options, of course, all of which we had tried. Some years we took the fifty pounds of dirty clothes to a commercial laundry, which finished the job in a few days. But that "solution" meant that we had to impose on someone else to pick the bags up and store them until our return, many months later. This was a real inconvenience to everyone because of storage limitations in Peruvian residences. We hated having to ask for this great a favor. One trip we paid Lichi's maid, Sylvia, three days' wages to do that last batch of summer laundry. Three *weeks* later we called Lichi to find out that Sylvia had only *just* finished the job!

"Why don't you just buy a dryer for the beach house?" my U.S. friends and family asked.

Well, until recently there *were* no gas dryers in Peru, only electric. At the beach, there wasn't enough electrical current to support large electric appliances other than refrigerators, so they were prohibited. And even if there was enough electricity available, the house didn't have sufficient space allocated in the utility area to accommodate an appliance that large!

At this moment I am sitting at a kitchen table in San Isidro wearing a black bra coupled with a bleached-out-yellow short-sleeve Old Navy knit shirt that I inherited from a friend of my mother. My hips are straining to fit into a pair of beige chinos recently borrowed from my sister-in-law, Lichi. Every single other piece of clothing we possess in Lima is hanging wet on three small lines in the covered patio just off the kitchen in Lichi's condo. If these pants don't stretch soon, I feel I might pass out. Then again, if they do, Lichi can gain ten pounds and still fit into them.

"How did I get into this situation," I ask. "Can't I even get dry clothes?"

In my other life in the U.S., even when all my other work-related and domestic endeavors failed, I could count on excelling as a laundress. In Peru, where *everything* ran counterclockwise, even simple tasks such as laundry became a major effort. I forgot trying to make a difference or even a point; I just wanted to be clean and dry again!

This particular laundry crisis began on our arrival from the U.S. on Thursday, when we found that the airlines had lost our largest suitcase. As we started heading south on the *Panamericana* on Friday, we received a call to our cell phone that the bag had arrived and was waiting for us in the Lima airport.

"We'll pick it up Monday," Jaime said, thinking we could make a two-day jaunt from the beach house to Lima and back.

As we intended to return to Conchitas promptly Wednesday morning, when we prepared our bags on that Monday, we packed lightly. A change or two of clothes would surely be all we would need for such a short trip. Jaime had the sniffles and didn't feel like packing much anyway, and I was in favor of not dirtying any more clothes, so each of us took one pair of slacks and a couple of shirts.

That Monday in Lima we did indeed regain the lost bag, which it turned out had been in the possession of the person whose bag we had accidentally picked up. Fortunately for us, some underwear and another top or two was in our bag, but there were no more slacks.

Jaime's sniffles turned into a cold, which brought on a fever and a cough. Monday turned into Tuesday. I read the only book in English I had brought with me, "Five People You Meet in Heaven." A wonderful book, but way too short. I stretched out and practiced tai chi – for hours on end. Tuesday became Wednesday and brought continuing fever and cough to Jaime. I slept on the couch, wore the same slacks, and walked several blocks to the nearest Internet café.

Our maid Doris arrived on Monday, thinking we were returning to the beach. Instead she found herself helping out Lichi's maid, because Sylvia had a case of the "burning heels." As Sylvia's condition was really rather painful, she went back and forth to doctors all week. The doctors were so concerned with and perplexed by Sylvia's condition that they gave her a mammogram. Results of the other tests came back negative, but the doctors had to wait to take other action until the mammogram results were in. Go figure.

Wednesday turned into Thursday and my one pair of slacks kept stretching by the day. By this time, they were dragging down to my hips, giving me the feeling that I lost the illusive last ten pounds all women strive to shed. Doris had come with only the clothes on her back, and by that time had been wearing them for two days. Lichi took us to a store that sold maids' uniforms to get Doris another uniform and some underwear. I still valiantly resisted buying any more clothes. Doris and Sylvia kindly agreed to sleep together in the maids quarters – head-to-foot in the same *twin* bed – which was against a wall that backed up to the kitchen of the adjoining condo. The neighbors had parties until late at night. Despite the crowded conditions, the girls claimed they could sleep well, at least after the parties ended.

My nights on the couch were interesting. Ear plugs blocked about one-third of the snoring and a little of the coughing going on in the other room, but none of the car alarms that spontaneously went off outside my window. I slept under a couch throw made of rustically woven wool that itched at night, but keeping my knees bent and pressing against the back of the couch relieved my hip pain and compensated somewhat for the lumpy cushions.

For days I dreamed of getting out of those slacks. The only dress I brought was sheer and I had no slip. It had belonged to my mother. Strange thing though, mother was several inches shorter than I was, but her skirt almost reached my ankles. For my feet, I had only black rubber thong sandals and old white jogging shoes. All combined, they made a fashion statement I didn't care to visualize. Most thankfully, the full-length mirror was in a closet in the room where Jaime lay.

Thursday became Friday, with little sign of relief for Jaime's cough or fever. I decided to take the major step of asking Doris to wash some clothes for us. Good enough, but then I wondered, "When would the clothes be ***dry***?"

A plan came to mind, "Why not use the large GE washer/dryer set belonging to Lichi's daughter, Ximena?" She lived just two floors above. Better yet, why not ask Doris to use Lichi's washing machine, which was smaller and slower, but located right here, and dry at Ximena's? Even better, why not avoid bothering Ximena and wait to use her dryer until their family left for a weekend at the beach?" It seemed like a sound plan.

I wore the dirty slacks, sending the other clothes off in the morning to wash, including our one set of PJs. Washing began in the little European-style machine – each load taking *six hours* to complete. By mid-afternoon clothes eventually appeared on the line. By late afternoon the clothes were still wet, so I changed out of my slacks and put on my mother's ankle-length dress, quite a sight with the white walking shoes. I asked for the key to Ximena's flat. No one had it.

"It is always here, but it was removed the other day by someone who needed to use her internet connection," confessed Sylvia.

I staggered back in disbelief. How could I get dry clothes without access to the dryer? In fact, no one knew why I had thought we would.

True, I hadn't actually *asked* anyone specifically about the dryer. Using it in their unoccupied flat had seemed like such an unobtrusive action.

"Just a minute," I said, beginning to shake, "I need to sit down and contemplate my wet-garment situation. What will we *wear*?"

There was a brief discussion of using Alexia's dryer down the street, but a call confirmed that it was broken. The possibility of outdoor drying was fading as fast as the sun. A commercial laundry was mentioned, but Lichi's car had just gone in for repairs, and no one knew if there was a laundry we could reach on foot – and if they would even take clothes that were already clean and wet.

"Better not ask," they said, fearing loss of face.

I was going to cry, but decided instead on a cup of anise tea. Lichi graciously produced a lovely embroidered white pima cotton night gown and a pair of close-fitting slacks.

The tiny, front-loading European washer with its indecipherable icons and no operations manual churned away at my back. That the maids knew how to use this was proof positive that employees are often times much smarter than their employers. My only pair of slacks was in there. In another several hours they might come out, perhaps in one piece. Then there would be the line drying, which would not quite be finished by tomorrow. If we left for the beach that day, what would we wear?

As I write this, the clock in the kitchen reads 9:30, the microwave 6:09. Since it is afternoon and still light, I'll go with the microwave. Tomorrow is Saturday and all sane people who aren't already at the beach will be there by noon. Whether we stay or go will depend on Jaime's fever and cough.

Whether we choose to stay at the beach after the weekend will depend on the availability of power and the electricity bill resolution, but that is another story.

During the first two *decades* of visits to Lima I learned how easy it was to lose the feeling of self in another country. This feeling of instability attacked the most basic survival instincts in my "reptilian brain," the part governing stimulus and response. Without the ability to take care of basic needs, like clean, dry clothes, it was impossible to feel secure in any way. Of course, it could not compare with real dangers, like those the Peruvians faced in the late 1980s, when we wouldn't have dared live that far from Lima. But those problems seem like they happened in the far distant past. Today's problems are more trivial, but as the Bible says, "Sufficient to the day are the evils thereof."

I learned the hard way that things I took for granted in the U.S., like access to machines to both wash *and* dry laundry, was in those days a priority reserved for maids in a few privileged houses in Lima. Over the years I had managed to adjust to spending every *hour* of our allocated vacation in Peru, staying in relatives' houses, with the resulting lack of privacy, change of language, no heating or cooling in the homes, having no one interested in what I did for a living, not being able to visit with my U.S. friends, a dramatic shift in the meaning of being "on time," constant traveling, and not being able to establish daily routines. The single issue I could not become accustomed to would be the lack of a washer and dryer for my own use.

Something had to give; and it finally did. The laundry situation alone took almost 20 years to resolve. It took buying a condo in Lima. But that is another book.

11

Our Maid Has a Nanny

It was a beautiful Easter morning. Jaime and I were at the beach house for the last weekend that summer. It was about 10 a.m. and we were sitting on the upstairs terrace off the second floor master bedroom suite, still in our housecoats, enjoying a beautiful ocean view. A new *techito* (pergola) had been installed over our second-story master bedroom patio, making it a very inviting observation post. The baby-blue sky was crystal clear, the ocean a deep dusty blue with gentle, white-capped waves. A cool breeze caressed our bodies. The beach was as quiet and peaceful as an empty cathedral.

For over an hour that morning, thousands of white birds called Peruvian Boobies migrated northward, flying to the right, like an endless stream of V-shaped waves. As they passed, a number of them happened to look down and see several large schools of fish. Suddenly hundreds of the birds, along with many large Grey Pelicans, decided to alight on the water's surface in circular configurations. Not to be outdone, small Peruvian fishing boats joined the party, and the whole thing turned into somewhat of a spectacle. There were five homemade *peque-peque*, as the locally-made boats are affectionately called, each with its noisy little motor and towing a rowboat. The nets they were casting were several times the length of each boat. I ran to collect the binoculars. Through them we saw a much larger boat, a *bolichera*, named the Carolina. It was freshly painted in blue and white. Its enormous black net was held aloft by a large white wheel crank and adorned with a ring of orange floats. Its crew of a dozen men was outfitted in orange slicker suits and hats.

While we were waiting for the net to be pulled in, our maid Doris came up to tidy up our bedroom. Instead of working, she stopped for a while to enjoy the ocean scene with us. In a Peruvian household this would be a rare event, as employers rarely visited with their employees. But as we shared the moment, I was reminded that Doris had time away from both her duties *and* her children because she had *help*.

Our maid had a nanny – and an assistant. It sounded a little strange to our friends in the U.S., where only the most affluent people had a full-time maid, much less one with a nanny *and* an assistant. It wasn't that we had ever intended to acquire a staff. I remember quite clearly when this all began last summer...

The previous January, I mentioned to Doris that we wanted to start helping her in some way when we were not around. Even though we were in Peru for less than a month most years, paying the annual social security and insurance benefits for her and her son seemed like a nice gesture. When I mentioned that we should register her for insurance during that same visit, Doris exclaimed, "Oh good, I need that now because I'm pregnant again!" She smiled radiantly – whether at the thought of her pregnancy or the insurance was unclear. Doris must have been confused too, thinking that a new insurance policy would cover her current pregnancy. Jaime and I certainly knew it would not. I began to see black clouds gathering on my mental horizon.

As she was unmarried, I asked her whether the pregnancy came as a surprise.

"Oh, no," she said. "And I intend to have another child after this one!"

Oh dear, I thought.

We had become so fond of tiny and energetic Doris, with her brown sparkling eyes, her dark cinnamon-colored skin, her long, wavy black hair, and her beautiful white teeth – not to mention her delicious meals! But, how were we to solve the dilemma of child care?

In previous years, when Doris was with us at the beach house, her son Paco, named after Jaime's father, stayed in Lima with a relative. When he was a baby, Doris had tried bringing him to work. His care wound up consuming much of her "working" hours. Things were even more difficult now, as he was a rowdy five year old. So we had started subsidizing the cost of a sitter in Lima in return for peace and quiet. But since Doris was going to have another baby, that solution had vaporized. By the next summer, Doris would have two children, one of them undoubtedly nursing, so an off-site sitter would be out of the question.

Before we could worry in earnest, there was the question of her delivery, which, if like the first pregnancy, must be by C-section. How could we resolve all this?

After consulting with the family, we found out that Doris' first child was delivered in *El Hogar de La Madre*, or The Mother's Home, a separate wing off of the hospital where a close relative had delivered her children. This special wing was set aside for employees like Doris, who had sponsorship but a significantly reduced ability to pay. The treatment, the doctors, and the medications were the same on both sides of the hospital. The only difference we could find was the floors: carpet or concrete. So arrangements were made: we would pay for Doris' prenatal care and for her C-section. We then turned to the question of child care for the next summer.

Doris assured us that she had a plan. "I'll invite my sister, Gregoria, to come down from her mountain village, to help us out."

"But doesn't she live *far* away? How long will it take her to get here?" we wondered.

"About 15 hours by bus. But she's made the trip before." Doris grabbed and reclamped her flowing black hair, as if to say she had this problem all wrapped up. "Gregoria can sit with the children in the maid's quarters while I work." Her eyes twinkled.

It sounded like a plan, but as we returned to Texas, we knew in our hearts that something would likely go awry.

Sebastian was born on September 1, 2001. We met him for the first time during our trip to Lima in October. Just one month old, he looked so cute in his little blue knit outfit, his thick black hair blowing in the breeze, and his left eye crossing ever so slightly. Seizing the moment, Doris asked us to be *padrinos,* godparents.

"But we aren't Catholic," we tried to explain.

Doris looked at us strangely. To her, this seemed both incomprehensible and inconsequential. We agreed instead to pay for Sebastian's schooling, uniforms, and supplies, for as long as Doris continued working for us. Then we returned to our jobs in Texas.

The following January we arrived at the beach house at 3:00 p.m., after flying in from Houston, picking up a borrowed vehicle, and making the hour-and-a-half trip south to the beach house. Doris was there waiting for us. The windows were spotless, cushions on the covered terrace were out and fluffed, the pool was clean and re-circulating.

Doris welcomed us with open arms and a big smile, "*¡Bienvenidos Señor Jaime y Señora Marie!*"

We all hugged, happy to see one another. From around the corner came Paco and Sebastian, who was in the arms of María, the babysitter.

"Where is Gregoria?" I asked.

 "She couldn't come."

"*Qué lástima*." What a pity. "Is María staying in the buildings near the gate as planned?"

"Well, no. The buildings at the entrance are the domain of Señor Gonzalez and we would have to ask him a special favor."

As Señor Gonzalez was one of our neighbors, we did not relish the idea of introducing this plan to him with no prior warning. So we acquiesced to having everyone at our house. Perhaps it could work.

"But where will you all *sleep?*" I wondered out loud.

"The maid's quarter is big enough. It has two bunk beds and a bath," she replied.

"OK," I acquiesced, silently vowing to stay as far away from that part of the house as possible. Two of our daughters were with us and we knew there would be no vacation without Doris' assistance. I had brought clothes for Paco and Sebastian. Doris was radiant.

Days passed. There was so little noise coming from the maid's quarters, which was located directly beneath the master bath, that we actually forgot that Doris and her entourage were with us. The only way we knew they were there was that excellent food kept coming out of the kitchen, clothes were washed, and the house was clean. This freed up our time and we were able to spend glorious days of leisure with our daughters. Life was good. The only problem was that our vacation was over too soon and we had to head back to our jobs in Texas.

We returned to the beach just five weeks later, for the last trip of the summer, bringing with us Bill, my dear friend and mentor. This time we drove directly from the airport to the beach, arriving at 1:30 in the morning. We were totally exhausted. Doris had arrived the day before, as had the food, sent by Wong Pedidos, a Lima-based grocery store delivery service. Fortunately for us, we were located within their delivery range.

Doris held little Sebastian, adorable in his second-hand sporty cap, sandals, shirt and matching shorts. His older brother, Paco, holding on to Doris' skirt, was also well-attired in more of the clothes we brought during the January trip. María the babysitter had returned. Then around the corner came Gregoria!

"What a surprise! When did she arrive?" I asked.

"Last night."

"What will she *do*?" Jaime broke in.

"Oh, she can stay with us to help out," assured Doris.

"But, where will you all *sleep*?" I wanted to know.

"In the maids' quarters." What a silly question!

"That makes five people in a room made for two!" exclaimed Jaime. "Should be interesting," he mumbled to me in English.

But it was by then 2:00 a.m. and we were all too exhausted to discuss the matter any further. Instead we simply wished each other a heartfelt *buenas noches*.

Sunrise came quickly and by noon the first of our guests had arrived. Jaime's oldest brother Jorge arrived early, bringing with him Diana and Enrique, two cousins who were born in Peru and now lived in Madrid and Paris, and their mother. Tía Chiqui, the youngest of Jaime's father's eight brothers and sisters, shuttled between her apartment in Madrid, houses of her friends throughout Spain and Scotland, and family homes in Lima and Conchitas beach. As a young woman she was as beautiful as a movie star and, even over 80, she was charming and quite photogenic.

Doris cooked and served lunch for ten people, a feat she pulled off without a hitch. After an all too brief nap and a beautiful sunset, preparations for dinner began. The house was ablaze with lights and the infinity pool facing the ocean shimmered with an aquamarine light.

Where lunch had been relatively quiet, dinner was another matter. Close family members began to arrive about 8:30 p.m., and by 10:00 p.m. there were 22 people. We started with *pisco sours*, followed by Argentine Malbec. Appetizers were *empanadas* (Spanish meat pies), toasts with goat cheese and sun-dried tomatoes, stuffed olives, and mixed nuts. Food appeared and empty plates disappeared in an endless stream. Brazilian bossa novas and the voice of Diana Krall floated through the air.

Doris and son Paco, the first year
she came to work for us.

Somewhere between Doris, Gregoria, Maria, and Jaime, an impressive dinner was being prepared. I never entered the kitchen. The *parrilla*, our large built-in patio grill, had been heated to perfection. Its entire expanse was laid out first with chicken and sausage, then tender beef filets, and lastly, with sweet red peppers and zucchini.

Dinner was finally served about 11:00 p.m. Food came and went, dirty plates were whisked away and clean plates and glasses appeared with each course. Dessert was a wonderful *volador*, a thin, crisp pastry, filled with creamy manjar blanco and apricot chutney, and dusted with powdered sugar. We finished off dinner with espresso, and chased that down with shots of Johnny Walker Black Label. At midnight I decided it was time to enter the kitchen for the first time that night, just to check to see if everyone was doing OK. Doris and her two assistants were hard at work. Maria had been washing dishes for several hours.

"How's it going in here, *chicas*?" I inquired.

"*Muy bien, Señora, pero estamos un poco cansadas.*" Of course they were a "little bit" tired, they'd been working non-stop for hours.

Outside, the guests stayed and talked until 1:30 a.m. After they left and everything was cleaned up, we all wished each other *buenas noches* and went off to our separate areas of the house. Tomorrow would be another day and perhaps another set of guests. We all needed some rest. Were there actually more guests the next day? Probably, but I don't remember.

"Oh, Marie." Jaime brought me back to our current reality. "Take one last look at the boat before it leaves."

Yes, the Carolina was leaving, taking with her a precious cargo of lively cold-water fish. We noted that she should have at least paid us a small fee for having taken so many fish from our waters.

"Say, how about a round of fresh fish for everyone on the beach?" I joked.

But before we could even begin to get her attention, the Carolina had departed for another fishing spot.

The next day the summer would come to an end for us. The pool would be drained and our house closed up for the winter. The pangs of sadness began setting in. It was the end of a busy but beautiful summer, and time to return to the "real" world of U.S. business: the world of rushed schedules, downsizing, acquisitions, mergers, and divestitures.

As I did each time we left Peru, I prayed that we would not let the corporate world, with its corporate priorities, drown us or change who we really were. I prayed that we would be able to return year after year to our house, with Doris and whatever troupe of assistants were necessary, to experience the peace of our own little country – La República de Conchitas.

There are those who might criticize us for having employees, but hear me out: in comparison to what all of our lives would be without these symbiotic relationships, this is a relatively good system. It works both ways: How else would Doris and other maids pay for their food, clothing, health care, and the education of their children? How else would we be able to entertain as much as is expected? If I didn't have Doris and her entourage, *I* would be the maid, but without the nanny – an unpaid servant in my lovely, open-air beach house, full of hungry guests. I challenge anyone to live and entertain in Latin America with no help at all.

Things are altogether different in our closed and temperature-controlled house in Texas. Over there I act as my own maid.

OTHER
CERRO AZUL

12

Lucky Tico

At our beach, we had the dubious pleasure of living next door to a five-bedroom home that was often rented. Most of the renters brought large families and stayed up all night playing games and drinking. But during March of 2001 a couple that I shall never forget rented the house.

They flew down from New York City to enjoy some South American sunshine during the cold North American winter. She was a tall, handsome, rail-thin blonde with flowing locks, whose pale skin seemed to have never seen the sun or enjoyed a mango. He was just the opposite, a slightly shorter, black-haired man of Peruvian Indian descent, who must have grown up on mangos. They were both in their mid-30s. The couple rented the house for just the two of them. We saw them often on the porch, and talked to them occasionally when they were under their *sombrilla* at the beach. I remember him in baggy flower-print swim trunks and her in a navy North-American-style two-piece swimsuit with boxer legs. They were a pleasant couple, enjoying the luxuries that can still be afforded in a developing nation – if you know where to look.

It was the Thursday of *Semana Santa*, Holy Week, when this couple decided to buy some fish. Their first thought was to go back to Lima. But prices for fish in Lima over that holiday weekend had soared to the astronomical sum of $10 per pound – and Lima was one-and-a-half hours drive to the north. No, they decided, it would be better to go to a village nearby. So they dropped by our house to ask for the name of a good place to buy fresh fish. We recommended the village of Cerro Azul, located about 15 minutes down the coast.

So they jumped in their rented SUV and took off south toward Cañete. At kilometer 132, where the *Panamericana* reduces from a divided highway to a two-lane road, they spotted the distinctive mustard-yellow wall with a double archway leading into the small fishing village. *Bienvenidos al Puerto de los Ensueños* (Welcome to the Port of Dreams), the sign read in bold blue letters. Barely avoiding being sideswiped by a large passenger bus, they made a sharp right turn and drove on the dirt road under the yellow arches and into the village. Houses were made of mud bricks, reinforced here and there with concrete pillars. Older houses were made of *quincha*, that ancient Peruvian construction technique where alternating layers of thin bamboo sticks are placed tightly together and covered with layers of mud. When it struck the fancy or the pocketbook of the owner, a few houses were painted.

In Cerro Azul, as in many other Peruvian *pueblos*, mixed-breed dogs of all descriptions lay in the streets. As the couple entered, two taxis stopped mid-street to wait for the dogs to pass. With this lax attitude, the prices for fish *had* to be lower than in Lima! The SUV wound around the dogs and the taxis, dodging people who crossed the street without even glancing up.

The couple passed the central flower-laden square with a concrete structure that resembled a lighthouse, brightly painted in blue and white. A dented blue 1954 Packard with a row of horn speakers on its roof announced special weekend events related to the upcoming holiday. Passing an abandoned hotel and beyond women selling herbs from carts in the unpaved dirt streets, they came upon a street lined with gaudy, brightly painted blue dolphin statues, some 30 of them in all. These new statues provided a ludicrous contrast to the condition of the rest of the village. The beach, with its fresh fish, could not be far away. The dolphin-lined street dead ended into a rope, casually draped between two *more* dolphins, the nose of which held a woman's bag. The apparent owner of the bag, a dark-skinned woman with shoulder-length black hair, wore a bright blue apron imprinted with the words Municipalidad de Cerro Azul, and was collecting parking fees.

"*Un sol,*" she intoned.

The couple paid their sol (35 cents) and drove inside. Beyond the rope, and to the left, lay a working-class resort. To the right lay the beach of Cerro Azul with its tourists and their colorful umbrellas.

"So this is the famous Cerro Azul from the song 'Surfing Safari'," the woman exclaimed. "How did the Beach Boys ever *find* this place?"

They drove straight ahead and behind some buildings to the fish market, easily distinguished by a pungent odor. The couple parked their SUV to the right of an unpainted *quincha* building, plastered with peeling political campaign posters, and disembarked. The beach in front of them was lined with locally-made *peque-peque* boats, each one about 15 feet long and painted with bright colors; some blue, some red, and others yellow. No sails or motors were visible, just oars. The boats, christened with names like Carmen, Santa Rita, and La Delicia, were turned upside down, as the fishing for that day had ended in early morning.

Near the beach was a long porch with a corrugated concrete roof. The floor was bare concrete, but the battered concrete pillars that held the roof had been recently painted bright blue. Two dozen fishermen were busy processing an enormous catch of fish. The air was filled with the pungent smells of spoiling fish juice and the sound of knives being sharpened.

Most of the fish caught that day were *toyo*, a fish that looks like a shark with no teeth. Their heads were cut off and their bellies slit open, with their innards thrown haphazardly on the concrete. Some were covered with ice, others were being "processed" inside large tires that had been cut open and lined with black plastic sheeting. Attached to the right of this porch was the fish market. The couple was surprised to find out that the highly praised "market" was nothing more than an open air grouping of six small concrete stalls with blue painted walls. Each stall was outfitted with a shiny white tile countertop and a deep sink with constantly running cool water. The slick countertops dripped a continuous stream of fishy water onto the concrete floor.

The fish market was unusually alive with people for 10:00 a.m. on a weekday. The couple wove their way through a group of men mending loosely-woven fishing nets made of forest-green thread knotted together and held up at the edges with various types of cork. Sitting just beyond them and to the left in little stalls made of *esteras* (straw mats) were people eating fish and drinking soft drinks and *chicha de jora* (a home-made alcoholic beverage that tastes like ginger beer). The *chicha* was served out of old plastic soft drink bottles and had the usual cloudy pale yellow color and distinctive thin layer of foam.

"*¡Muy buen toyo!*" a woman cried, "*¡Chita, corvina, lenguado, perico! Desde quince soles el kilo.*" (About $2.50 a pound.) Now that was more like the price for fish! The couple bought 1.5 kilos of *lenguado* (flounder) and two-and-a-half kilos of that queen of South American fish, *corvina* (sea bass). They asked that it be filleted and that the head and *espinazo* (spine) be placed in another bag so that their maid could make *chupe* (a hearty fish soup) one night.

Waiting for their fish to be cleaned, the couple noticed the large number of stray dogs lounging around, every one of them a mutt. The dogs fell into two basic categories. The first group was a collie-mix, spotted black and white or beige and black. Most of the others were small, perhaps a terrier mix. All the dogs were covered with fish juices and fresh sand. One limped. The thought of these dogs biting one of them made the couple cringe, but the dogs seemed not the least bit interested.

Then, all of a sudden, a tiny Pekinese-mix dog swept by. He was about a foot long and six inches at the shoulder, easily the smallest dog on the beach. He had a long, thick shiny brown coat tipped in black, big brown eyes, floppy ears, short legs, and a long curled-up tail. With only the slightest glance in the direction of the fishermen, he grabbed a fish fin and pranced off to the beach to enjoy his "catch."

"¿Cómo se llama ese perro?" the couple asked a woman who sat next to the fish processing area, eating a bunch of grapes.

"Tico," she said, *"Como el auto."* Tico is the brand name of a small Korean car that was sold in Peru for many years. Cerro Azul was full of old Tico taxis, in various states of disrepair.

The couple watched the little dog, becoming increasingly enchanted with his peppy disposition, light-hearted manner, and small size. "What a pity that such a cute little dog should have such a hard life," they said to each other.

After talking it over, they decided to do what they considered a very charitable thing; take little Tico back to live with them in the U.S. There he would have all the advantages of any North American dog. What dog could want for more? So they called to little Tico and invited him to go with them in the SUV. Tico was delighted. What fun to go for a ride! Tico was so small his head barely showed out of the back window as the SUV drove off away from Cerro Azul and back to Conchitas beach.

We enjoyed watching the couple and Tico. Each morning he was there with them as the maid served breakfast on the patio and later each day at the beach, catching their bright orange Frisbee and bringing it back, no matter how hot the sand got.

All too soon the couple found their vacation coming to an end. After doing some research, they found that getting Tico out of Peru and into the U.S. would be much more of a problem than they had imagined.

"But why?" they asked. "Who would want to keep a little stray dog in such a poor place? The Peruvian authorities should be grateful to rid their country of another unwanted animal." Nevertheless, between the Peruvian authorities and U.S. import restrictions, the couple lost the better part of three days in Lima and more money than they cared to admit. So much for a peaceful end to their vacation.

"But it was all worth it," they assured themselves. "Little Tico will be the luckiest dog to have ever been born in Cerro Azul."

With their vacation over, and with Tico freshly groomed and in tow, the couple left Peru and returned to New York City. Having used up almost all their vacation time, the couple had to return to work immediately. The plane arrived in JFK airport at 7 a.m. By 10 a.m. they had dropped Tico off at their apartment, showered, changed clothes, and headed off to their offices.

At first Tico was so tired from the journey that he just slept. But it was not too many hours before he began to sense an acute feeling of loneliness, hunger, and a pressing need to go to the bathroom. He quickly looked around the small apartment. There was nothing to eat, drink, and there were no appropriate places to use the bathroom. Sniff around as much as he might, nothing gave a clue that another dog had been there before him. Tico began to fret. He must have wondered where this new place was and how he could he get out. As the day wore on, the need to urinate became so urgent that Tico finally relieved himself on the corner of the sofa and on the living room drapes. He appeased his hunger by chewing on some high heels he found in the closet.

After the sun set and the apartment became very dark, the couple finally returned, exhausted, from their first day back at the office. Their joy in seeing Tico was quickly overcome by a powerful smell and the realization that some of their furniture had unpleasant yellow stains. Tico saw their expressions change from joy to anger.

"Bad, *bad*, dog!" they exclaimed. Then they slapped him on the nose and stuck his face in the yellow stains. "Don't _ever_ do that again!" And that was before they saw the high heels.

Tico was now not only hungry and thirsty, but his spirit began to break. Immediately he was taken outside and shown the proper places to go to the bathroom, if he should ever be so lucky as to be allowed outside again. It was cold and dark and the wind was blowing from the north. The couple had tied some sort of noose around Tico's neck and they followed him wherever he went, tugging at the noose whenever he found evidence of another dog. They used a scoop to pick up anything he left behind. Tico looked back at them, as if to say, "What a strange practice!"

As the months dragged on, very little changed between Tico and the couple. They got their furniture cleaned and Tico learned to use the bathroom on his rare trips outside. And after a while he stopped pulling against the noose around his neck and pretended to ignore the picking up of his droppings. Each day the couple would leave the apartment as the sun began to rise. As soon as the door closed, Tico would jump on the couch, which he was forbidden to get near, and up on the back so that he could watch them catch a bus going in the direction of downtown. There were times when the couple left Tico at another location with the smell and sound of strange dogs. There he was locked up in a little cage for days with only moments to go out to the bathroom. Tico especially hated these times. To let them know his unhappiness, he would avoid the couple for several days after they returned, and sometimes leave little "reminders," so they wouldn't leave him again.

Tico and the couple never really understood each other. If he was the luckiest dog in Cerro Azul, he certainly didn't feel like it. The couple felt he was an ungrateful mutt, who could probably never change. They debated leaving him at the local pound, but being good people, they were not ready to abandon little Tico so far away from his home. They agreed to make another trip to Peru in August and take Tico back where they found him.

And so it was that the couple and Tico arrived in Cerro Azul one cloudy winter day in August 2001. No loud speakers blared and the taxis had taken their hopes for business elsewhere. But as they went through the brightly painted arches, Tico's nose picked up the scent of the fish and the ocean's salt spray and he began to jump up and down, whining and scratching at the window. Could it really be that, after all those months of loneliness, he was back in his own hometown! The thought was almost too good to be true.

Seeing Tico's reaction, the couple realized that they were doing the right thing. They parked at the fish market and were almost overwhelmed with the scent as they got out of the car. When they opened the back door, Tico was so excited he leapt out, landing with his face in the sand. He picked himself up, shook off, and ran straight for the fish stalls. Grabbing a fin that had been carelessly dropped, Tico headed out to the beach where he played with other dogs, rolled in the sand, and chewed at the fin to his heart's content. He never looked back.

The couple watched Tico with a lack of comprehension. How could this little dog, which they had given the best they had to offer, prefer a poor, smelly fishing village to the largest city in the U.S., where he could share with them both security and a promise of a safe and temperature-controlled, albeit somewhat boring, life.

Shaking their heads, the couple returned to their car. As they drove off, they tried to avoid talking about what might become of little Tico, with no owners, no veterinarian, and without the knowledge of where his next meal was coming from.

"How lucky we are to have our priorities straight," they thought.

The next day they boarded the airplane that would take them back to New York City and to the bonuses, the retirement plans, and the stock options that came with their secure jobs in the World Trade Center's Twin Towers.

By late March 2002 we realized that the New York couple would not return to rent the house next door. Whether they had lived through the bombing of the Twin Towers, we would never know. In truth, we were afraid to ask. Feeling sad, we returned to Cerro Azul in Easter 2002 to buy fish and to look for Tico. Could he have survived another year?

Heading for the beach, we saw women and girls in half of the stalls, hawking fish. The other stalls were clean and washed down. Some men were down at the beach with their boats. There wasn't much business, as the fishing for the Easter weekend was complete and the relaxation had begun. The usual entourage of stray dogs was there, but there was no sign of little Tico. How sad.

After purchasing our fish we headed several blocks away to the town square to buy some flowers at the Florería Rosa. While we were haggling over the price of two dozen deep red roses, who walked in but Tico! The owner greeted him, and from the tone of her conversation it seemed that Tico had been able to successfully negotiate himself into a very comfortable situation. I started to speak to Tico in my best "doggie"

Spanish, to break the news that his adoptive family would not return. The minute Tico heard my voice he sped off to the left, behind the sales area, and into the kitchen. Without regard to the fact that I might have been invading private territory, I followed him behind the counter and through a passageway blocked off by the remains of a white patterned shower curtain.

There he lay, facing in the other direction. He was spread flatly across the floor, tail slapping the concrete and legs sticking out on both sites to absorb as much of the coolness as possible. I tried to speak again, but when I did Tico's tail stopped moving. In order to see me without moving his head, Tico turned his huge, brown eyes so far to the side that it seemed as if they would pop out of his head. Further talking only caused Tico to try to flee deeper into the house. I then realized that he no longer trusted the judgment of people who spoke English and who said they meant him only good. He seemed not the least bothered by the lack of veterinarians and owners with pension plans and stock options.

Perhaps Tico understood what we often times seem to miss: that the only day worth living is today and that there is no place as safe and as comfortable as your own hometown.

A few years later, the gynecologist who so poorly constructed that vacation home sold it to two lovely and unsuspecting sisters and their families. One of the families lived in New York. Although they were not the original subjects of this story, I continued to follow the progress of both little Tico and the New York co-owners. The husband was self-assured and well-to-do, being involved in maritime oil transport. It was he who gave us an early warning that the price of oil was about to skyrocket. He stood to make a lot of money, which would have made him a happy man if it weren't for a pain in his stomach. I advised him to see a doctor for some tests, which he did upon returning to the States. But by that time, his hidden colon cancer had metastasized. We were devastated to learn that he died shortly thereafter, at age 53.

That next summer, I returned to Cerro Azul and to the flower market. While waiting for the owner to finish arranging a batch of white gladiolas, I almost fainted when in walked none less than Tico – alive and well! He had outlived them all.

Tico finally died, about a year afterward, of pneumonia. Had his *Yankee* benefactors outlived him, I'm sure they would have taken him to a vet.

13

An Angel on the Beach

I slipped out of the bedroom and down the *lajas*, the white flagstone stairs covering the open air staircase that led from our bedroom, across the little bridge to the guest house second floor, and then down the entry staircase to the main patio. The sun had not yet come over the mountains and an eerie light permeated the air. Heavy dew covered the patio, creating the impression that the tiles had just been waxed. I made myself a cup of cappuccino and moved to my writing desk in the downstairs bedroom.

My memory drifted back to the first days of Conchitas, a time when only a few adults appeared on our intimate horseshoe beach. These were the days before the first families acquired their permanent *sombrillas*. Those early days were the building blocks of what is becoming an established beach; one with friends we share our lives with, summer after summer.

If memory serves me, it was our second summer that children began to appear on the beach. Among the first houses constructed were three similar homes built at beach level; brothers flanking either side of an architect. Three baby boys were born to the families either side of the architect's house: to the left there were the twins, blond-haired Rodrigo and brown-haired Nicolás, and on the right side their fair-haired cousin, Alejandro. We first noticed these three when they were barely old enough to walk. All three played on the shore with their parents, joyfully digging in the sand. They would run back and forth along the sunny beach, shrieking with joy. In those days, the twins had matching blue print swim trunks. Their slightly older cousin, Alejandro, nicknamed "Ajo," played along with them. They looked like triplets.

Friends remember that, as he grew older, Ajo would sometimes go looking for a flower to take to his mother. Being on a desert beach, there were no wildflowers, so Alejandro would go to a neighbor's house asking for permission to cut off one of their red geraniums. With this, he would head happily home, his mother's gift in hand.

Another year passed and in January and March we were again at the beach. The twins had acquired a little wagon packed with a plethora of beach toys. Back and forth they would transport this wagon, one pulling and the other pushing. Somewhere in this timeframe, they were joined by the lovely granddaughters of the "Suizos," a family of Swiss descent who lived high on the rock bluff overlooking the ocean. Little Ajo, looking paler than usual, now sported a bright red cap. He seemed to run less than the others, but was always eager to meet new people. Neighbors fondly remember him coming up to anyone he didn't know and introducing himself with, *"Soy Ajo."*

We heard through the grapevine that the reason Alejandro always wore his cap was that he had cancer and had lost his hair in his chemo treatments. As we looked into his little face, the blue eyes looking back belonged to someone whose age was far beyond his years. Still, he played in the sand and walked along at the water's edge, just beyond the reach of the others. During his many treatments, he always asked to come back to Conchitas, where he thoroughly enjoyed the beach.

I still don't know just when it happened, but one summer day we headed down to the beach to enjoy the view. The twins were playing in the surf with their new turquoise and tomato colored "boogie" boards. Thinking I was carefully sneaking photos of them with my camera, I caused them instead to run away yelling "No. No." I looked for little Ajo with his white skin and red cap. Look as I may, he was nowhere to be seen. Did I dare ask...?

Cautious inquiries confirmed my worst fears. Our prayers had not been answered in the way we had asked them to be. While we were back in Texas, little Alejandro had passed away. In their sorrow, his parents rented their beach house and to this day have never returned. Though his family was gone, we knew that the spirit of little Ajo would remain.

Surfers in training, the first members of Conchitas' next generation pull their "boggie" boards towards the ocean.

Each year we returned, the twins grew bigger and stronger. They ran faster and pushed their "boggie" boards further into the surf. This April they will be six years old. They now have little interest in their wagon, with its multitude of toys. They occasionally recognize me and some days I receive a salutatory kiss. Too soon they will grow up and the little girls running beside them with their beautiful tans and their tiny bright blue and green bikinis may become more than just friends. It will all happen too fast.

After writing these lines, I rose from my desk and looked out past our patio, perched mid-level up the hill, past its pots of red geraniums and past our rock-faced retaining wall with its brick-colored bougainvilleas spilling over the ledge. In the misty morning light I "saw" a tiny angel in a red hat, joyfully playing on the beach. He was running back and forth along the shore, with a broad smile, dancing and waving his little outstretched arms.

For many of us, the memory of little Ajo will never die. As we grow old, he will be forever young and forever with us.

I don't know if our neighbors can see him, but look, look down there! Surely you can see that little red hat...

How often I have waited for just the right time to have a good life. Little Ajo didn't. By simply living, he left our beach community with an indelible image of what it means to be fully alive. Ajo's death did not make us forget him. To us, he became immortal.

As I was wrapping up this book, something uncanny happened. A beach ball sitting by itself in front of what had been Ajo's house began moving on its own. It made the rounds of all the houses he used to visit, and then it moved downhill to the *sombrillas*. Suddenly it reversed direction and traveled *uphill* – back to his house. No one felt the breeze that must have carried it.

While we can't say with certainty that Ajo came to visit us, some of us believe he may have done just that.

14

En Route

"Where can we buy clay wall sconces?" Jaime and I asked Ana Teresa one day while we were building the beach house.

"You don't know about Hofita's place?" she exclaimed. "Everyone knows Hofita. I'll take you there." We jumped into the car and drove a few miles north of Playa Asia.

Located precisely at kilometer 86.5 on the *Panamericana* south of Lima and north of the remains of the second toll booth, is Cerámica Hofita, an establishment referred affectionately to as "the pot place." To the uninformed motorist this looks like an ordinary roadside pottery stand, though slightly larger than most. It is easy to spot from over a mile away, not due to its prominent sign, but because of an enormous inflatable Coke can perched precariously atop a tall pole.

Although we've been going up and down the *Panamericana* for many years, no beach vacation is complete without stopping at Hofita's at least once. Something inside me always cries out, "What can it hurt to just drop in and see what's new?" Fortunately for us, Hofita's place offers an unending variety of affordable shapes, most created from the same reddish clay. We often say to Hofita's wares, "Of dust you were born."

Hofita sells pots, both of cement and of *barro* (clay), in every imaginable size and shape, many with optional plates. Shapes range from conventional to downright eccentric. There are the urns, some the shape of those in ancient Rome, others with clay fruit flowing down the side. There are concave pots, convex pots, pots with holes throughout that don't hold water. Among my personal favorites are those shaped like animals, such as the stacking frogs that appear ready to reproduce, or the smiling Indian women with large open holes in their stomachs, always ready to accept seeds or to sprout new life. Hofita also carries old *pisco* pots and fermenting pots for the Peruvian favorite, *chicha de jora*, that foamy yellow alcoholic beverage I have yet to get up enough nerve to taste.

Tired of pots? No problem. Hofita has many other wares to try the imagination. There are foot-long clay creations in the shape of fanciful fish, some of which serve as candle holders, and there are the clay wall hangings in the shape of marlin, dolphins, and parrot fish, many of them painted fantastic shades of brilliant orange, blue, and yellow. There are the usual and unusual variations on candlesticks, always handy in a place where the power goes out with unpredictable regularity. There are wind chimes in a variety of shapes, ranging from abstract to dancing dolphins, flowers, mushrooms, leaves and twigs. There are several variations on the cuddling sun and moon. One of the unpainted versions, with a smooth quarter moon cupped closely against the smiling and radiant sun was so irresistible that it now hangs on an entry patio wall of our beach house.

There are wall sconces in a wide variety of shapes. Most have open tops that support the light bulb business by allowing for maximum bulb corrosion. Oddly, none of the sconces are painted. "Let's buy some of those," I said pointing to a conical sconce. We took home a dozen or more that day. Later we added layer upon layer of white paint to the ones in our beach house, along with a layer of frosted glass on top.

Hofita has stylized figurines ranging from three see-no-evil-hear-no-evil-speak-no-evil Indian women, to nativity scenes, to votive candleholders with scenes of Peruvian towns. There is a whole section of bizarre yet realistic professional representations, from the dentist pulling a man's tooth to my personal favorite – an obstetrician giving a partially clothed woman a C-section while seated in a chair.

You can also buy a few plants, mostly cactus and bougainvillea, and *abono* (natural fertilizer). Occasionally, I find an angel. It's a good thing, because we'd need one soon enough.

"We're organizing a trip to Tacama!" Tere announced one day. "Our friends are renting a large van. Want to go with us?"

"It's not going to be like that trip we took with Lichi years ago, when the van broke down several times on the highway, is it?" Jaime and I responded skeptically. That was some years ago, but we hadn't forgotten the van full of our Peruvian and U.S. family, stuck way outside town, sweltering in the heat, and swatting flies while the driver told us the vehicle would need some days to repair.

"Oh no, I'm going to hire a *new* van... with air conditioning." Tere said. "*No te preocupes.*" (Don't worry.)

Tacama, one of the oldest vineyards in Peru, is widely recognized as one of the best. The only reason we hadn't visited it earlier was it was located several hours south of the beach house and a long day trip. But renting a van would relieve us of making that long journey alone.

"OK, count us in," we agreed.

On the designated day, we waited patiently in the dust at the entrance to our beach community. Minutes dragged on and on. We used our Peruvian cell phone to call Tere's cell, "Where *are* you?"

"Oh, one lady had an important appointment and was delayed. She's getting out just now. We'll be there soon."

After over *two hours* wait in the equatorial sun near a blue-ringed light post, we saw a late-model aquamarine-colored van coming over the horizon. When we got in, we found it filled with the matriarchs of families who owned some very important businesses in Peru. They were "dressed down" in the latest styles of cotton and linen casual wear with strappy sandals, sunglasses, and beach hats. Though few wore any jewelry, some wore their diamond tennis bracelets and one had forgotten to remove her multi-carat marquis-cut diamond ring.

We headed south past Cerro Azul, where little Tico still lived, and then on through the fertile Cañete valley, with its six-foot tall pima cotton plants, and the dusty town of the same name. As we left the valley and headed uphill into the desert, we were stopped by the police.

"Where are you going?" the patrolman asked.

"To visit the Tacama winery," replied the driver.

After the usual check of the driver's license, insurance papers, and title, the policeman gave our driver a stern warning. "Whatever you do, don't drive through this stretch of road after sunset. There have been a lot of robberies just south of here. There are new land invasions. Watch out because we've seen some of the thieves put rocks in the road. When drivers stop to remove the rocks, they are beaten and robbed. Cross this stretch during the dark and your lives could be in danger!"

We drove off, a bit shaken as Jaime and the driver were the only males in the group. As we entered the desert south of Cañete, we saw thousands of *casas de esteras,* shacks made of woven straw mats, many flying the Peruvian flag, scattered along miles of hilly desert. The sudden appearance of *estera* shacks are a familiar but unwanted sign along the Peruvian countryside. During my early visits to Lima, I assumed that these were built by desperate people, fleeing to Lima to escape the terrorist tyranny in the mountains. Not so, I would soon discover. There is an old law still on the books in Peru that says that *anyone* can lay claim to a piece of unoccupied land, regardless of who owns it, if they can erect a house on the property. What was undoubtedly meant to give everyone a place to build their houses has provided a business opportunity to unscrupulous "land developers." What look like slums are actually appropriately named *pueblos jovenes* (new towns). Most of these will, over a period of many years, become towns filled with partially-finished brick buildings.

A future *pueblo joven* begins as a piece of undeveloped land. A "developer" selects the land because it is conveniently located, but not guarded. He creates a drawing of the area, complete with numbered lots, locations for future schools and other public areas. Then he sells the lots to the unsuspecting poor for $1,000 or more, promising to provide land titles, utilities, and social services. The sad truth, the new owners soon discover, is that the developer invariably disappears without providing any of the above. Thus the often-repeated terms *estafado* (cheated) and *estafador* (a person who cheats others).

Whether the *estera* shacks are occupied depends on the convenience of the location. In this case all the shacks seemed to be unoccupied, but the nearness of many shacks to the *Panamericana* gave thieves a perfect place to hide.

"We'll definitely return before dark," the driver assured us.

As we reached the half-way point on the journey to Tacama, still deep in the desert, the engine started overheating, forcing the driver to turn off the air conditioner. Seated in the first row, we could see beads of perspiration forming on the driver's furrowed brow. I happened to glance at the temperature gauge. It was rising precipitously. As the women in the back sang Peruvian folk songs and groused about the heat, Jaime and I began to fear a repeat of our previous van adventure.

When the burning sun hung straight overhead, and with nothing but enormous sand dunes as far as the eye could see, the van sputtered and stopped. The driver got out and opened the hood. Steam rose in clouds as he added a bottle of drinking water. We resumed our southward trek, windows open to the breeze. The ladies stopped singing and began reciting the Rosary. What seemed like hours later, we made a sharp left onto a small unmarked dirt road. Once out of sight of the road, the driver pulled the van into a large hedge of purple grapes and asked us to get out.

"*Señoras*, the van won't go any further," he said. "There is a restaurant back down the road. You can get something to eat there. I'll be back as soon as I can."

The ladies donned their beach hats and sunglasses and eased out of the vehicle and down the dusty road. There was indeed a restaurant, *La Olla de Juanita* (Juanita's Pot), complete with its own *pisco* bar and grapevine covered porch. We wiled away the hours there, sharing our tales of family, travel, and various "youth enhancing" products and procedures, until the driver returned with the van.

We arrived at the back entrance of the Tacama winery just as they were closing down for the day. A quick discussion with the guard about exactly *who* was in the van quickly opened up the gates for a special after-hours tour. As we walked through the centuries-old winery, we passed the *hacienda*.

"That's one of the houses Tía Lucha decorated," Jaime exclaimed. He recognized it from some of his godmother's photos. It seemed Tía Lucha had connections everywhere.

We finished up at Tacama late in the afternoon and climbed back into the ill-fated van. There was a cool breeze, turning cooler by the hour, so we had no need for the air conditioner. The sun was setting as we entered the vast expanse of desert hills that the policeman had warned us about so many hours before. The van was beginning to jerk.

Oh dear God, keep this van going, just a little while longer, I prayed. The other passengers were silent. The ladies were no doubt also appealing to the Higher Power. Then, just as we crossed the last bridge, leaving the desert, the van jerked wildly. Feeling the inevitable descend upon us, I yelled to Jaime, "Hold on, we're gonna FLIP OVER!"

There was a loud "BAM" and the van listed heavily to the left and skidded sideways, as we saw sparks flying from the right hand side of the van. We landed half-way over into a row of bushes on the roadside. It was pitch dark. We were terrified.

"Out of the car everyone. *¡Adelante!* This van could blow up any second!" the driver exclaimed. A squealing rush of cotton, linen and purses squeezed out the front door of the van. But once outside, what were we to do? We were standing on the side of a lonely road, in the deep of night – sitting ducks for any robber or kidnapper. The driver had bigger problems, seeing immediately that we had lost not only a tire, but an entire *wheel*. After a lot of searching in the dark, he found that it had rolled down into the river we just crossed. He came over to us, head bent in shame. "*Señoras*, I'm afraid that is the end of the van for this trip. You'll have to find another way home."

"*¡Ay, qué tal día!* (What a day!). Do you think we'll *ever* make it home?!?" exclaimed one woman, her diamond tennis bracelet obscured in the moonless night. We all inhaled deeply and I saw many women crossing themselves.

Just then, a large bus of indeterminate origin, with a sign that read El Melchorcito, pulled over onto the shoulder. When the driver opened the door, it was the most welcome sight we'd seen that whole day. We quickly hopped aboard.

Each person has her own idea of what an angel looks like. I always expected to see a glowing figure surrounded by an aura of bright light, with shining blue eyes and blond hair flowing in the wind. But for us, on that dark and scary night an angel came with dark hair, dark skin, and black eyes. He smelled a bit of perspiration as he opened the door of El Melchorcito, the bus that carried us back into our own limited version of reality.

To those uninitiated in Peruvian culture, this may not seem like a strange site but, trust me, it was. These women had never been on a bus in their lives; they wouldn't even be caught dead in a taxi. Many of them had their own chauffeurs, so a local bus full of farm workers was a real unknown. I wondered what the workers thought of all the linen and diamonds. Would they try to rob us?

Though they may have had private thoughts, the humble, dark-skinned workers made no sound as they kindly moved over and made room for the ladies with the diamonds and light skin. All of us felt terribly out of place – intruding into other peoples' lives.

When we reached the town of Cañete, the bus stopped and street vendors came aboard, hawking their wares. *"Camote, chicharrones, lonche..."* The sweet potato and roasted pork fat sandwiches brought on board smelled strongly of some unpleasant combination of herbs and animal grease. I held my breath as the workers ate their dinners, washing them down with the much-loved Peruvian soft drink, Inca Kola. Finally the meals were over and we were on our way again.

"Señor," we addressed our rescuer, the bus driver, "would you be able to stop at our beaches and let us off?" This was not normal, as that

bus only made scheduled stops, but the driver, seeing our distress, kindly consented.

As we neared Conchitas I pulled out my cell phone. After that eventful day, all I wanted was to get back to the peace and security of our functional home – and to the nice dinner Doris could have waiting for our return.

"Doris, you won't believe the incredible day we've had," I began. "I'll tell you all about it when we get there. Please start dinner. I'd love to have some *caldo de gallina* (chicken soup)...."

"*Señora*," Doris interrupted, "there's something you should know. *¡No hay luz!*"

The electricity had gone out again. All I could do was laugh out loud.

Up and down the *Panamericana,* and other Peruvian highways and byways, I have learned that there are some things that everyone can count on: power outages in rural areas, non-potable tap water, the flexibility of time, and the utter unreliability of rental vans. I also learned that the things I feared most, like being stranded in the dark on a dangerous stretch of road, were not that terrifying when they actually happened. I stopped being as afraid of the unknown and began enjoying life a little more, trusting that when we really needed it, God could send us an angel. It all made for a great story – further down the road.

Conchitas beach provides privacy, unparalleled ocean views, and from some hilltops, a night time view of the distant lights of Playa Asia. Unfortunately, unlike Playa Asia, Conchitas beach has not yet provided a steady flow of electricity to its houses.

15

An Early Autumn

"If I stay, I die!" was the troubled explanation that a fellow employee gave for leaving a successful scientific career with our company. He packed his things, got on a plane bound for his Pacific-rim country, leaving his wife, my co-worker, to sell their lovely lake-front home and give away everything they owned. What had happened to this brilliant Ph.D. and scientific researcher? I would soon find out.

Our Continental flight landed at Lima's Jorge Chávez airport with a thud. It was midnight and the air was clammy and smog-filled. Exhausted, we dragged our suitcases towards a waiting taxi. It was early March.

"Ah, we're back in Peru at last. So far away from our stressful jobs! We've got two whole weeks to rest up before going back to the rat race." I remarked to Jaime.

Staying in La Molina, we rose early the next day and enjoyed a typical Peruvian breakfast of *pan francés*, with its characteristic crisp crust and soft center. Ana Teresa's maid Irma had set out butter, strawberry jam, an assortment of fragrant cheeses, thinly sliced ham, and *café pasado*, a liquid coffee extract. Doris arrived and we packed up our little grey Peugeot and headed down the *Panamericana* to the beach house. We drove over desert hills of golden sand and charcoal rocks, both as dry as the surface of Mars. Then we headed through river valleys lush with apple orchards and fields of grapevines, red roses, luscious green asparagus, aromatic cantaloupe, and brilliantly-colored bougainvilleas spilling over rough-hewn brick walls. About 24 miles south of Lima, we drove straight into rolling clouds of marine mist that looked like flocks of lost sheep searching in vain for grazing lands on the barren Andean foothills. Then the *Panamericana* descended, revealing to our right the vast Pacific Ocean with its waves glistening in the sun.

"Look at the size of those waves! They must have eaten away a yard-high ledge of the beach." The infamous *maretazo* – rough seas – had arrived, a month ahead of schedule. Although summer officially lasts through Easter, to the coastal residents that phenomenon heralds the end of the season.

"Summer can't end now. Our vacation has just begun!" I cried.

Jaime and I had dedicated our lives to working for a Fortune-500 chemical firm for the past 30 years. Though I worked as hard as I could for first 25 years, my job description could have been wrapped up in one word, "Underutilized." But the past five years things had gotten much better. Thanks to the challenging corporate environment and one boss who believed in me, my responsibilities expanded and I became a global consultant for my fields of expertise. However, just when our jobs were becoming more diverse, a massive corporate "downsizing" began, stripping thousands of people of their jobs. As we lamented their early departures, we prayed to be allowed to complete our own retirement points, which we would get that year.

Things at work were not good. The unique jobs Jaime and I created had reached suffocating impasses: we'd accomplished 95% of our goals, and the phantom 5% that remained was untouchable. To make it worse, the organizational structure above our heads was disintegrating. My wonderful, supportive boss had just retired and a new manager sought to cut costs by denying services. It felt like I was falling into a sink hole.

At the beach, I wondered, "What will be left of our jobs when we return?" Then thought again, "We almost have our retirement points, so staying on after the age for early retirement has few rewards."

"Retirement is definitely on the horizon, but when?" Jaime remarked. "After that, then what will we do? I can't see us starting all over again in outside consulting jobs. They require too much travel."

"Yes, we want to be together, not on the road all the time," I said, "Traveling was fine for a time, but I can't keep up that pace anymore."

I reflected back over the trauma of the past few weeks...

Although I sat on the board of a local charity clinic, and have always been concerned for the small, the poor and the weak, my new boss at work demanded that I dramatically reduce the scope of those I helped with their business improvements.

"Reduce the areas you support to the 15 largest sites," he commanded.

"Please identify which ones," I asked, since site size could be measured by headcount, pounds of product produced, expenses, profits, or maintenance costs.

There was total silence from the other side of the desk.

I continued pleading my case, "But I support over 150 sites! What am I to do with all those other sites? They are so poor – so forgotten."

"Let them sink or swim! What concern is it of yours?" he shouted.

Caring for the underdog had been a hallmark of my career. I could not abide this!

The end of my working life occurred toward the end of a lengthy teleconference. Our group had been sitting for several *days* in a windowless Texas conference room with poor ventilation, talking to our fellow department members in western Canada, via a black box, when I began a descent into the black pit of despair. I remembered that feeling all too well from the darkest days of my divorce decades before, when I lay on a bed, curled up in a ball and unable to eat. The only word I could say for days was "naught." As if to say: All my years of loving work had come to nothing – nothing at all.

But the pit of despair *had* returned and I broke down during the meeting, crying uncontrollably for hours. In my 30-year corporate career, nothing that humiliating had ever happened. The remarkable thing was that no one around that large, U-shaped conference table even noticed my collapse. One man was kind enough to pass a box of tissues my way, but our new boss – who had promised to make a lot of changes – continued his verbal attacks. Two hours later, I closed my laptop, got in the car, and cried all the way home. Jaime, hoping to shake my mood, drove us to Houston, 60 miles away, where I cried all the way through a lovely dinner. On the way home, I was *still* crying.

About 10 p.m., I began hallucinating. The attack lasted well into the night. After hours of delirium, I finally passed out in the early hours of the morning. The next day I couldn't see through my left eye and I began to fear the "black hand" of retinal/vitral detachment that my right eye had suffered during a terrifically stressful period two years before. In the months that followed, I was ill all the time. Tests revealed that my immune and lymphatic systems were failing. I was so confused and disoriented that driving was almost impossible, especially on business trips. I began to understand the statement, "If I stay, I die."

While in the U.S. I had pleaded with those around me to allow my early retirement, but no one was sympathetic. "How can you leave? You'll lose some of your pension," was the oft-repeated answer of my family and mentors. But I was absolutely desperate to exit this irresolvable situation.

Fortunately, a brief vacation to Peru and the beach house was just around the corner

Once we got to Conchitas, I vowed not to return to my corporate job. Seeing no other way out of my dilemma, I scheduled an appointment to kill myself for 9 a.m., the last Thursday in March. A special cliff, down the road from the beach house, was calling me. "Just a quick jump and down to the rocks below," it said.

"They say the first step is always the hardest," I laughed hysterically. It is clear now that I had gone quite mad. But how could I be mad when I'd even figured in time for my body to be recovered and a quick Peruvian funeral before Jaime's scheduled return to his all-important job in the U.S.? To show how rational I was, I told Jaime of my efficient plan while sunning under our *sombrilla* on the last Monday of our vacation. He made no comment whatsoever, but on my scheduled Thursday morning I found us back in Lima, far away from the cliffs.

Having survived that brush with death, I could see it was long past time to adopt a different perspective. No job was worth this. If I was to remain among the living, I had to take another road.

Jaime was persuasive, "We've paid off our house and car loans, educated the kids, saved for retirement, and even renovated our house." Referring to our new status in the family, he reminded me with a smile, "Don't forget: we're now 'Papapa' and 'Grandmarie'. If we are going to enjoy our lives, we'd better do it now."

And so we decided to live, love, and look for new directions. I systematically prepared to shed the global role I created. With the new boss and his restrictions, it was too heavy a cloak to bear. I worried, "Will my job be rent into pieces and distributed to others, or will the areas go unsupported?" My summer side stressed, "How will the dream survive?" "Let it pass," my autumn side answered, "If Management doesn't care, why should you? Take a deep breath and *let it go*."

Looking through the beach house *mamparas*, a large black and white Kelp Gull glided serenely by at eye level. As it turned its head my way, I could almost hear it say, "Let it go."

During this period, Jaime picked up his guitar after a break of over three decades. In those years, families had been created, torn apart and remade, grandchildren had been born, and loved ones departed. He played every morning and evening; his music was the salve that mended my broken heart. Juan Carlos and Nino, two other members of the VIPs, a once-popular Peruvian rock band, came to visit and brought their guitars. Only this time they were acoustic, not electric guitars. Instead of the rock music they played in the springtime of their lives, they were now playing romantic boleros and '60s ballads.

We were not alone in our quandary. Other family members and friends were also "in transition." The interesting jobs and accompanying rewards were no longer being offered. The possibility of advancement was gone. On the excuse of corporate necessity – not age, of course – one relative had his salary, but not his hours, cut in *half*. A family friend returned from vacation to find her office emptied and in the hallway – a younger woman had been offered it the week before. Another friend who worked in Human Resources survived months of overseeing layoffs only to be told that he then must fire his *own boss*. Questionable ethics were everywhere. Whatever the consequences, we could no longer be a part of that world.

Jaime argued, "Look on the bright side. We're lucky we can retire early. Under Peruvian law, retirement is not possible until age 65. We'll be the envy of all our friends. We're blessed to have had two incomes for 30 years, along with our pension plans, 401K accounts, and personal savings. What more do we want?"

"But we *are* our work. If we retire, who will we *be*?"

To take our minds off weighty life-changing decisions, Jaime's oldest brother, Jorge invited us to a theatrical performance of mammoth proportions. *El Gran Teatro del Mundo* (The Great Theater of the World) was a passion play written by an acclaimed ancestor, Pedro Calderón de la Barca. The evening of the performance was still and cool. Entering the Plaza de Armas, we found ourselves walking beside the internationally-known Peruvian author, Mario Vargas Llosa. I remembered that in his book, "Aunt Julia and the Scriptwriter," his main character said that a man reached the perfect age in his 50s. From the viewpoint of that decade, we could affirm that this was true.

We settled in on bleachers for the historic performance. The cast of several hundred included the National Ballet, National Choir, 21 horses, and a group of costumed actors who performed their parts on stilts. This play had been held annually in the heart of Lima since the mid-1600s, being acted out on the steps, the façade, and the roof of the cathedral. In the play God, *"El Autór,"* sent each heavenly being to earth with a different role: a king, a rich man, a beauty, a nun, a laborer, and a beggar. In heaven they were all equal; only their assigned earth roles were different. Each played his or her assigned part, some with kindness and others without mercy. After each death, they returned to heaven to be judged on how well they played their role. Relating that to my current situation, I realized that we were all just acting in a *play,* and would ultimately be judged not by our earthly success, but – scene by scene – by how honorably we played our part.

Changes were surely coming; the signs were everywhere. The brick-red bougainvilleas that climbed the walls of the Conchitas house and those that cascaded down the terraces felt the change. Despite frequent watering, their blossoms began to dry up, turn brown, and fall off. But their root system was sound and ready to regenerate during the cloudy Peruvian autumn and winter. We knew they would burst forth with new blooms next spring and summer.

On that trip, we found that our beloved beach house, built like a fortress on a hill just six years before, was in need of some repair. Despite the use of the best river sand and concrete, mixed with the purest water, a supporting column showed signs that the steel rebar was corroding. To avoid damage to the structure, this column had to be torn down and rebuilt with new, more flexible materials. So it was with the institutions that supported our lives. We had to change.

The blazing summer sun was softer those days. I leaned over the tempered glass wall of the second-floor master bedroom patio. A cool ocean breeze rearranged my hair and caressed my checks and arms. I stood alone, inhaling the fresh air, and gazing into a crystal clear day. I felt that I could see *forever*.

Playa Asia to the north, with its thousands of houses, was clearly visible, as was the table mountain of Pasamayito with its clean-sliced opening that permits the four-lane *Panamericana* to pass through. Looking in closer towards our house, I saw Sarapampa, that beautiful, flat, undeveloped beach which belonged to the local indigenous people. Next there was the beach being developed by Navy retirees, with its partially constructed pier. Even closer there was the YMCA beach with its tiny houses and unkempt tents, which were fortunately well out of view. I could not see the cove of La Escondida, the hidden one, with its few houses well out of site, but clearly visible was the Isla de la Gallina, the chicken island, a rock which I focused on while meditating.

If I was going to retain my sanity and my health, I had to return stateside with this breathtaking view in my heart.

That weekend there were more fishermen and fewer home owners at the beach, perhaps because school had begun. Of the residents we saw, deep bronze to mahogany tans displayed the rewards of basking in the 12 weeks of Peruvian summer. We were fortunate to have been there for six of those precious weekends, ourselves nicely bronzed. The surf was up and the surfers with it. Our neighbors were down at the beach, catching the rays of a late summer day. The day was developing into something out of a story book.

Jaime called from downstairs, "What are we waiting for? Let's get the snacks and head for the beach!"

Once down at the beach, everyone gathered in awe as several large dolphins came so close to shore that they were within a few feet of where we'd just been swimming. They were riding the waves and leaping out of the water – for sheer joy, it seemed. Knee-deep in the blue-green surf, we cheered and clapped as the dolphins jumped into the air. As if in response to our exuberance, the show continued for what seemed like half an hour. Eventually the dolphins headed northward in search of lunch, and we found ourselves drawn together, talking to some of our neighbors for the first time.

That evening there was an unfamiliar stillness in the air that called us to a sunset dip in our infinity-edge pool. Longing for one last candlelight dinner, I called out into the kitchen, "Doris, please set the table for dinner on the terrace. *Con velas*."

Jaime poured us a drink, "Just think, after we retire we can make two trips a year instead of three and stay for several *months* at a time."

"I dream of having time to *think*, to write, to walk in the sea breeze and soak up the sun. No more windowless offices!" I shouted.

"But don't forget we'll be living on less income. That reminds me, we've got to file our income taxes and schedule a visit to our financial advisors as soon as we ..."

Catching ourselves mid-conversation, we whisked away those heavy thoughts, clicking our wine glasses together and changing the topic.

Jaime put on José Miguel's romantic *Inolvidable* album. The night was full of stars. A half moon shone over the Pacific, illuminating the water and the waves that broke on the beach over 100 feet below. The blue glow of the infinity pool was calling us back out onto the patio. Spontaneously, we began to dance.

The hard work of the summer of our lives was coming to an end and an early autumn, with the relief of retirement, was on its way. I shed a tear for the passing of the summer. But autumn was a new beginning, the harvest awaited!

When the CD finished, Jaime pulled out his guitar and we sang together a piece the Carpenter's sang so many years ago:

"And when the evening comes, we smile..

So much of life ahead

We'll find a place where there's room to grow.

And yes, we've just begun!"

Planning and saving for retirement was like dropping our hopes and dreams – and even pieces of our *souls* – into a slot on the top of a locked treasure chest. Retirement gave us the key. We took that key, unlocked the lid, and began peeking inside. Who would we *be* after retirement? Time would tell. What we knew was that we would be *together* in all our adventures. We learned to enjoy each day and to guard our *health* so that we were ready for whatever treasures life held down the road.

Jaime and I retired on the same day, May 31st, driving together past the guarded security gates that had marked the past 30 years of our lives. Sick and exhausted, we slept for 14 hours a day all through June and July. One day in June, hiding out in our air conditioned house from the sweltering Texas summer heat, we were startled to receive a phone call from Veronica, the maid who handles beach house *limpieza profunda*, the heavy cleaning. We knew the situation must be serious because Veronica had never called us in the U.S. before.

"*Señor* Jaime," she sobbed. "Something *terrible* has happened. I didn't do *anything*, I swear. But when I went upstairs to clean the guest rooms, I found shards of broken mirror all over the place! I didn't do it, honest," she pleaded. "That huge wall mirror in the bunk bedroom just fell off the wall and shattered."

How well we remembered that 3 x 4 foot mirror. It was expensive, imported, and had been professionally bolted to the wall. Ever since the mirror broke in my Samsonite makeup case on the way to my first wedding, I'd felt that mirrors that broke spontaneously did not cause bad luck, but were meant as a sign. But what sign could it be? I shuddered to think what this meant. Since no one had given us the mirror, I couldn't link the sign back to the donor. It must be what the mirror was reflecting... the bunk beds. I thought, *Something terrible is going to happen to the one who watches over the children!* But as mother had never visited the beach house, I didn't think about her health.

Less than two months later, in early August, my mother called to say that she had started throwing up all her food. Mother was 85 and we had thought in perfect health. But she met her match with undiagnosed Stage 4 colon cancer. Jaime and I postponed our September return to Lima, due to Mother's condition.

When word of Mother's pending demise got around, hundreds of people my parents had befriended over the years came to pay their last respects. The guests continued at such a pace that my parents left the front door open and there was a line outside. Jaime ran a sort of ad-hoc restaurant, cooking not only the foods Mother had avoided all those years in the name of health, but meals for out-of-town visitors. Despite Mother's prior warnings against Latin men, she repeatedly exclaimed to anyone who would listen, "My son-in-law is an *angel!*" But it was Mother's last words that broke my heart. Looking in my eyes, she said, "I've got to go now. You should already be in Peru." Then she went into a coma and passed away two days later.

Jaime and I headed for Lima soon after Mother's funeral. On the way to the airport, we got a call from the funeral home saying that her ashes were ready to be picked up. Unable to turn back, we phoned a friend, who graciously offered to do that auspicious task for us. My sister, Eileen, would see to the headstone placement.

We would have to wait to bury mother's ashes until we returned to Texas – in late November. The tables had turned. Now I was the one who was not available to my loved ones in their hour of need.

16

Jorge and the Five Loaves

Jorge is the oldest of the five brothers and sisters. A top graduate from law school, he is a manager for a large Lima-based textile firm. Jorge speaks several languages, among them Spanish, German, Italian, Latin, and English. He even studied in Germany for a year. The tallest of the siblings, Jorge stands about 5'10". He is in the best shape of the three brothers, exercising vigorously every day. With his dancing eyes, broad smile and great sense of humor, when Jorge gets involved things happen. Jorge is indeed a ladies' man – it is just that the ladies he keeps company with these days are all as they say, *mayores de edad,* um – older.

Jorge is known throughout our extended family for having a big heart. Although he never married, or perhaps because he didn't, Jorge loves to be at family gatherings, which, of course, always involve food. Although he regularly attends these functions, his capacity for reciprocating "in kind" is limited, as he is single and lives alone. He has a lovely, but small, condo high in a building on the *malecón* in Miraflores with a million-dollar view of southern Lima and the Pacific Ocean.

Jorge has always more than compensated for his limited capacity for entertaining by providing a myriad of other kindnesses. He is the family member most known for his special concern for the oldest and the youngest generations of the family. Being a lawyer and fastidiously fiscally responsible, in the years since we decided to build our beach house, Jorge is *the* person we rely on for keeping our accounts straight and coordinating work – from house construction to maintenance issues, even paying our employees. Jorge was usually the first person to read my memoirs, correct their errors, and provide me with further insights. And it was Jorge who translated and distributed many of them to the extensive family network. Before I begin this, let it be understood that we all *love* Jorge.

When we arrived in Lima on New Year's Eve, we asked Jorge if he were coming soon for a weekend.

"Of course, but not until February," he answered. "In January I'll be in Miami."

Jaime thought out loud, "We'll have Jorge for a quiet family-only visit. I'm not sure what we'll do..." I shuddered as I recalled the first weekend Jorge spent at the beach house many years ago.

As was his custom, Jorge had brought dinner rolls as his contribution to the food. That Saturday, I had planned lunch for Jorge, Jaime, our maid Doris, and me. I'd made one small meatloaf and had set aside two heads of broccoli to boil and four Roma tomatoes for slicing.

"We've got plenty of food," I assured myself.

However, as lunchtime drew near, Jorge returned from his morning walk. "I invited a few family and intimate friends from the beach," he informed me with a casual smile. "*No te preocupes.* No need to worry."

As lunchtime approached, I peered out the kitchen pass-through window to see 15 people sitting around the patio! They all looked hungry. I panicked and did what every red-blooded *gringa* would do – I popped a cork on a bottle of merlot and poured myself a glass – then another.

Jaime came into the kitchen. "Why aren't you out there mixing with the guests? They're all asking about you. Is there something *wrong?*"

Feeling my face flush, I replied, "Wrong! I'll tell you what's *wrong!* How in the *world* do you expect me to make *one* tiny meatloaf, *two* heads of broccoli, and *four* small tomatoes into a dinner for 15 and still find the composure to entertain all these guests – in *Spanish*?" My heart was racing.

Jorge came in, all smiles, his palms invitingly held upward and out. "Isn't it *wonderful* that everyone I invited decided to come?"

I could stand it no more. "*IN THE UNITED STATES OF AMERICA,*" I began lecturing him, in English, "it is an *obvious* breach of etiquette to invite guests to *someone else's* party! *Everyone knows* its *common courtesy* for the hosts to invite the guests and *no host* would invite more guests than there were places to sit them or food to feed them!"

For a full half minute Jorge stood there staring at me, his mouth open in stunned surprise. He eventually regained his famous charm. Smiling, he replied, "But, as the old Spanish *dicho* says, '*A la tierra que fueras, haz lo que vieras.*' When in Rome..." My customs were not valid here. We were in Peru, not in the U.S. Never mind it was *our* home. Speechless, I glared back at him, hands on my hips.

Inhaling deeply, pursing his lips, and smiling politely, Jorge raised his eyebrows, shrugged his shoulders, made an about-face, and went back to the party. He didn't seem to grasp what I was saying. I turned back to Jaime, shouting, "I'm going to stay in *this kitchen*, drinking *my merlot*, until you either *get me out of this mess* or I pass out!"

Dear Jaime stayed and worked with Doris to do something creative to expand the food. I did my part and kept on drinking. To this day I don't know what we all ate. I seem to recall a lot of bread. Perhaps Jorge, being the most devout of all of us, was able to make his five loaves multiply. But that fiasco had occurred years ago. Perhaps things would be different this time.

On February 1ˢᵗ, we received a call from Jorge regarding his upcoming weekend visit with us. "How fortunate we are that Tía Teresa will also be at the beach that weekend!" he exclaimed.

Quiet, genteel, and amiable, Tía Teresa was one of Jaime's paternal aunts. Mother of six grown children, and grandmother of many more, she was the honored and adored matriarch of her large clan. We reflected that only 15 days before, La Tite, as we called her, had lost her beloved husband, Tío Bruno. Tite would be staying with her brother Mimo and his wife Carmen at their neighboring beach house the next weekend.

Jorge inquired carefully, "Could we invite the three of them for lunch on Sunday?"

"Of course, we'd be delighted," I said.

Later that day we got another call from Jorge. "What did you think of asking some of Tite's children to drive down from Lima to have lunch with us on Sunday?"

"Why not?" I said. "We've been planning on doing this for some time. You can call for us, Jorge, and invite them." I could almost see him smiling.

Counting immediate relatives on his fingers and two toes, Jaime replied, "Looks like we'll have about 12 for lunch."

The next day Doris, Jaime, and I were on the way to buy food for the weekend at the large farmers' market in the town of Lurín. To the casual tourist, Lurín looks just like any other dusty Peruvian village, but we knew differently. Lurín was the location of many beautiful homes and expanses of green equestrian training areas for the famous Peruvian *Caballos de Paso*, walking horses. It had an extensive open-air market with meats, fruits, and vegetables. It also housed some of Lima's best plant nurseries. Perhaps to keep tourists from overrunning this paradise, everything of interest was behind walls with closed gates. All a visitor could see were the dusty, hole-riddled streets filled with dirty, ill-kept *micros* and moto taxis.

By the time we arrived at the Lurín *mercado*, Jorge had called three more times, raising the number of invitees to 18. Some of the children were bringing their children, but they assured me that each of the young ones would come with a nanny and their own picnic lunch. Tite's oldest daughter had volunteered to bring *empanaditas*, delicious Spanish meat pies, for snacks. Wonderful.

Leaving the Lurín market, we drove south down the single-lane, shoulderless, pothole-ridden old Central Highway to find a *vivero* (nursery) selling small lantana and *hiedra* plants, a variety of geranium. The 30 pots of *hiedras* at the beach house no longer flowered. The impending luncheon prompted some swift remedial action, and Santos, the gardener, would be there that day to plant them.

By this point our little grey '95 Peugeot was loaded to the window tops with food, suitcases, flowers, and a new iron-bottom drawer for our extra large outdoor grill; the old one having just rusted through. Sitting in the passenger seat with my lap full of groceries, I gazed at the road ahead through a roof-high bouquet of blood-red gladiolas, perched on the floor between my sandal-clad feet. As we poked and bumped along, all I could see past the crimson blossoms was the back end of an old truck belching black smoke and struggling with an overload of red onions. I consoled myself, "It's only a mile to the entrance to the *Panamericana*. Looks like we've survived another trip to the market."

Just then a man jumped into the road waving and shouting, pointing to our right front tire. We drove past him, suspecting that this might be a trick. Within 100 feet, another man waved us down. This one was wearing an official blue Repsol gas station jumpsuit.

"What's going on?" Jaime wondered. "He has a uniform; this must be for real."

Remembering a previous trip, where we ignored the warning signs and wound up with three destroyed tires, we thought it better not to get caught with tire trouble in the middle of the *Panamericana*. Just the memory of that trip, coupled with the thought of all those groceries spoiling in the equatorial sun, the flowers wilting, and hundreds of buzzing flies appearing from nowhere, was enough to make me dizzy.

So we stopped for the neat-looking man in the royal-blue Repsol jumpsuit, with thick black hair and smooth cinnamon-colored skin. "I saw your wheel shaking. Something may be going wrong with your tire. Let me check." He knelt down and looked at the wheel with real concern.

"How lucky we are," I exclaimed, "to have come upon this guy just at the right moment!"

The man in the Repsol suit got down on his knees and juggled the wheel back and forth. He reached behind the tire and produced a mangled piece of black rubber with a hole in the center. "This is broken, I'll have to go back to the gas station for parts," he said. "It's down the road. You can drive me there and save us all some time." The problem was we had no extra room in the car. About then, we noticed the man's assistant walking down the road toward us. I volunteered, "Doris, why don't you and I stay behind? There isn't room for all of us in the car, along with all these groceries and flowers." As we were getting out of the car, a highway patrol car drove up and parked beside us.

"What seems to be the problem?" the patrolman asked.

We recounted our situation. To our surprise the patrolman said, "Drive a bit down the road and back again. Let me check out your car."

The men in the Repsol suits started walking slowly away. "There's nothing wrong with your car," said the patrolman. "But there have been a lot of robberies of people who later recounted a situation just like this one." The police officer drove quickly after the men, captured them, and escorted them into the patrol car.

"How can we thank you for saving us from those thieves!?!" we asked the policeman.

"*Pues,* you could help us out with some gasoline money," was the quick reply.

Jaime thought 20 soles (about $7) would do. And so it did.

As we pulled away and turned onto the *Panamericana,* we congratulated ourselves again on our good fortune. "Can you believe the timing? We were saved from highway robbery by a guardian angel patrol. And it only cost us $7." Then we thought again. "That cop sure smiled when he got the tip; perhaps it was all part of a well-practiced charade."

"Oh well, we are safe and just think, now we can recount another 'near miss' adventure that cost us a whole $7." We all agreed. "If we make it through alive, it was an adventure."

In defense of the police, we have since talked with several people who have assured us that those men in the Repsol suits were indeed real thieves. They told us that the thieves always work in groups of three. The first man to point to our tire was in on the scheme too. Had we left Jaime in the car with the thieves, we might not have seen him again, in the same shape anyway.

When we finally arrived at Conchitas, we got another call from Jorge. It seemed that one of the children wanted to bring her *novio,* and then there were the two very close friends – just like family. I ran out of fingers and toes to count on. Another call a few hours later prompted us to grab a piece of paper to write down all the names. We were getting confused.

"It looks like we'll have about 30 people for lunch," estimated Jaime.

"But how can we know for sure?" I wondered. "It could be even more!"

"Thank goodness we have Doris, who can handle these fluctuations," said Jaime.

The next day was Sunday, the day of the luncheon. Jorge went out for his morning walk. Anxious memories of our first Jorge luncheon began creeping into my head, but I attempted to push them away. Lunch was at 2:30 and it was already past 11:00, so I entered the kitchen to check on Doris and her progress. Since Doris had so efficiently taken over the cooking some time ago, the kitchen had become foreign territory for me. Doris wasn't there, but in the sink was a large soccer-ball-size sack of frozen chicken breasts.

"I will never understand why Peruvian maids freeze all meat unless it will be eaten the same day it was purchased. Even worse, why do they wait until just before a meal to thaw it out?" I asked Jaime. "It's maddening!"

But there was no time to waste. I found a large pot, filled it with cool tap water, and dropped in the frozen soccer ball. No other food was in sight. Doris entered, covered in perspiration from mopping floors.

"Why did the floors need mopping today instead of cooking lunch?" I called out in English to Jaime, who was intently cleaning the pool.

"Well, we'd better get to work," was all he said

"What have you planned for appetizers?" I asked.

"There are the *empanaditas.*"

"Yes, but is that enough for 30 or more hungry people?"

"How about tuna salad?" Jaime knew he had me there. Tuna was always my first choice.

We had asked Doris to pre-prepare a green bean salad with feta and roasted pecans, but she was still mopping floors.

"Help!" I cried out loud to anyone listening. "The guests will be arriving soon."

Feeling the tension, Jorge wandered into the kitchen with a tentative smile, "Is there anything I can do to help?"

"Go to Tío Mimo and Carmen's house and ask to borrow her maid," I begged.

Off he went, returning in almost no time with Violeta, a jolly woman who was always happy to help us out, as well as enjoy our food. She went to work finishing the cleaning. During his brief visit, Jorge had found out that Tía Teresa was bringing her life-long maid, Oti.

"With these three maids, we might survive the day," I hoped.

Beach regulations required that a list of all guests be submitted ahead of time to the front gate, but there were too many invitees to make a simple call. We had submitted a computer-generated list that morning, but the names kept changing. So Jaime updated the list again and took it to the guard. Yet even after that, the number of people continued to change. We gave up trying to keep track of them all.

With Doris finally in the kitchen, work began in earnest. About 12:30, Teresita arrived with Oti, carrying two boxes filled with tiny, delicious *empanadas*. One friend had not come, but another did, and he brought a large *tortilla de patatas*, a rich and flavorful Spanish potato pancake. Others who had planned to come along with them had, at the last minute, decided against it. The list began to shrink.

When Oti and Violeta joined Doris in the kitchen, we began to relax and to pack for the beach.

Down at the beach we hauled all the accoutrements to our assigned spot in the sand: the next-to-last *sombrilla*. But we quickly noticed that since the tide was out, everyone was at the water's edge, some distance away.

"Where is our group?" I asked Jaime, frantically. Scanning the water's edge, we finally noticed some familiar faces and went over, greeting everyone with salutatory kisses.

"We have food under our *sombrilla!*" we volunteered, and off they headed.

The *empanadas* were a great success, as was the beer and other snacks. We went back to the house a couple of hours later, empty handed.

Back at the beach house, and to our pleasant surprise, food kept arriving with each carload of guests. The amount of wine and especially carbonated beverages could have stocked a small store. What I had worried might not be enough food kept multiplying and the number of guests shrinking until the proportions of need versus availability reversed themselves. In fact, after we had all eaten our share, enough tuna salad, *ají de gallina* (the famous Peruvian dish of chicken and local peppers), potatoes, rice, tomato salad, green bean salad, and *tortilla de patatas* were left to feed another six people!

How many were there for lunch? Maybe 22. In the end, the number of guests didn't matter at all. What did matter was that abundance overcame need, as has happened so often in the autumn of my life. How blessed we were.

"Now, who will we invite to share our abundance *next* weekend?" Jaime asked.

Over the years I have learned that we cannot really *plan* for how many people will come to large events. We use the rule of two-thirds attendance versus RSVPs and get pretty close. I no longer worry about there not being enough food.

The same is true in life. How many times have I worried about not having enough savings, enough clothes, even enough space in the car? Usually I wind up with too much of whatever it is. Just as in the parable of the loaves and the fishes, I know now that when people share what they have, there is always enough.

17

Pleno Verano

It was mid-February, exactly the middle of the Peruvian summer. We were in the period called *La Canícula*, coming from the Latin word "*canis*," or in English, canine – thus the term "dog days" of summer. In the northern hemisphere, this period occurs between July 21 and August 23. In the southern hemisphere, it corresponds to January 21 to February 22. In Peru, the end of this timeframe is sometimes referred to as *Pleno Verano* – the fullness of summer, and brings with it an incredible explosion of both good and bad energy. I am reminded of the movie "Like Water for Chocolate," where we were warned about the danger of lighting all the candles at once. But on this part of the Pacific coastline, that is exactly what people do. During a period of one or at the most two weekends, there is a huge explosion of energy.

The hoards of renters with their non-uniform temporary umbrellas placed to strategically block the ocean view from our *sombrilla* had departed, and the owners began to return. Owners who came to the beach for as little as a week or two a *year* showed up for this very weekend. The beach community returned to its peaceful state, with just the residents and their guests.

The twins, who once played so happily with little Ajo, were growing up. It seemed that we watched them grow several inches, just this summer. They never lost their passion for riding the waves. This summer they graduated from "boogie boards" to new, "soft" surfboards, one tomato red and the other turquoise. They greeted us with a kiss and proudly showed off their new boards, made using the latest safety technology, complete with rounded ends and removable rudders.

At one neighbor's house, a multi-faceted contingent arrived from Miami to enjoy for the first time ever their spa/entertainment center, which was in effect an entire second house attached to their main house via a glass catwalk. As in previous years, they were accompanied by a posse of chauffer/bodyguards, an otherwise unknown quotient at this beach. Why they would need them, we chose not to ask.

Other neighbors had just returned to their expansive summer home, which occupied the entire hill just below our house. For the first time that summer, we saw the cadre of servants, as they unloaded supplies for the guests filling their ten bedrooms. These guests, in several Lexus SUVs, a Jaguar convertible, and a Porsche Boxster, must have arrived during the night. We counted a dozen cars in all. We watched as one of their sons arrived in his flame-red Jaguar. As he got out of the car with his two little children, I cried for joy that he looked so well. He had just returned from a lengthy stay at M.D. Anderson, the cancer hospital in Houston. His leukemia was in remission, giving him time to enjoy the rest of the summer.

The tide of the summer had begun to change. Only the day before we had heard news that a warm El Niño current was on its way and could raise the ocean temperature by six degrees. With the ocean temperature rising to a warm 65 degrees Fahrenheit, the habitats of the marine life and the birds would completely change. That day, for the first time that summer, we once again saw thousands of sea birds flying from right to left in myriad V-shaped formations. As in previous summers, they were on a feeding frenzy, following schools of fish that must also be migrating south. Perhaps the timing of this migration had something to do with the incoming warm current.

Jaime's family began arriving at our beach house for a gala weekend visit. Ana Teresa and Paco were with us, as they had rented out their beach house that month. Jorge was scheduled to arrive on a Soyuz bus. It looked like we were in for a wonderful time.

But little things started going awry. When I answered the doorbell, there stood Jorge, but with his pants ripped in multiple places and blood covering his legs, due to a bad fall exiting the bus. After recovering from that shock, I returned to the kitchen to check on the apple cake that usually cooked in an hour, but was still moist in the middle after two hours. Cooking longer only resulted in terminal burns to its bottom. I took a spatula and chiseled it out of the pan. But time was passing so quickly that there was not a moment to fret over lost opportunities. We had to catch the *wave* of energy or it would be lost. The sun abruptly disappeared behind the clouds without warning – a phenomenon that almost never happened in *Pleno Verano* – and was replaced with a cold wind; a bad omen for sure.

Doris had made a wonderful *asado* (pot roast) for lunch. Unfortunately, my body no longer digested this combination of ingredients and my stomach began to expand like it would explode. Time for an Alka-Seltzer. On that unfortunate day, however, this did not abate the cramps, so I took to the bed.

"Roll over on your stomach," Jaime suggested.

"But it will give me wrinkles." Then I thought again, *Who cares, if I'm not around to see them.* I rolled over. We both took an hour's nap.

Doris left during that time to attend Mass, as did Jorge and some of our guests.

We awoke an hour later to a loud *BOOM*. Then there was silence. The ceiling fan stopped. "Oh no, the electricity has gone out," Jaime exclaimed.

A trip down the sidewalk revealed that the improperly-run underground wiring of the neighbor's new spa house had short circuited. The explosion left a gaping hole beside the glass catwalk between their two houses, and the entire beach without power.

"We are so lucky that, with all the skylights, our house doesn't need much electricity," said Jaime. But this close to the equator, the sun set promptly at 6:45.

Jorge returned from Mass with the setting sun. Fortunately *té*, the name for a light dinner, was not until 7:00 p.m. As luck would have it, with nothing else to do without electricity, our guests arrived early – a phenomenon previously unheard of in Peru.

Nightfall came quickly. Then it began to "rain," a rare event indeed. Our tiled patio was filling up with little puddles of water, making it very slippery. Walking around in the dark was Tío Mimo, who turned 85 that year. I was afraid that he might fall. But to balance out that bit of negative energy, we had a guardian angel: one of our guests was a young and beautiful female medical student and she gladly took on the task of watching out for him.

Better get dinner together. "Oh Doris! Where *are* you?" I called out in the dark.

Silence.

"What are we going to feed everyone?" I privately wondered. "Better get busy. Boil water for tea. OK. Take the Burgos cheese out of the black hole of the refrigerator. Feel around – it was in a drawer. Light a candle or two, if you can find them in the *despensa*." I entered the walk-in pantry and retrieved the candles, but they didn't provide enough light to prepare dinner.

I wasn't concerned about dessert, as Carmen had brought a large *alfajor*, made of thin layers of pie-crust-like dough filled with *manjar blanco*, a thick milk custard. Then there were the remains of two of the ill-fated apple cake layers, which I could sprinkle over ice cream, but what else were we to eat? The young medical student offered to help out. I wonder if she had brought with her any anesthesia, which would put me out of my imminent misery.

Jaime was outside talking to the guests and did not notice how dark it was in the kitchen or the difficulty I was experiencing getting dinner together. He came in to find an ever-tensing wife.

"What's wrong?" he asked.

"Well, we could start with *no* Doris, *no* lights, and *no* menu," I responded crisply.

Jaime found a flashlight, which quickly vanished in the crowd. Carmen and the medical student helped set the table. Still there was no food.

"Jaime. Help!"

But Jaime had returned to his Martin acoustic guitar to serenade our guests with some 16th Century Peruvian Baroque music. Perhaps for him this moment of impending darkness and a living room full of guests was one for contemplation. But there in the pitch-black kitchen, I felt no such comfort, only an oncoming attack of hormones, as my temperature began to rise unnaturally.

We bumped into each other in the dark as I was taking out a plate of appetizers.

"Would you hold my guitar while I do something?" he asked innocently.

"What I want to do with this guitar is hit you over the head!" trying to get my point across. Perhaps in the dark he couldn't see my expression.

"Let's go upstairs and talk," he suggested, employing his best crisis management skills. Good idea. Away from the guests and the guitar.

After our upstairs chat, Jaime headed out in the car to look for Doris. He found her blissfully visiting in the dark with the maids from down the street.

"Do you know what time it is?"

"*Pues, no.*"

"Did you notice the sun set about a half hour ago? We have a house full of guests!"

No comment.

Jaime gave Doris a ride back to the house. By the time they arrived, I had pulled something together for dinner and had a buffet set up. Still, the cleanup would take another hour. Doris' services, as always, were indispensable.

In the end, everyone ate their fill. After dinner, all the guests joined together to sing everything from Peruvian coastal folk songs to Mexican drinking songs, with Jaime supporting us on his guitar. But the darkness took its toll. With no electricity, the guests left early – about 10 p.m. – a first.

As we headed back to Lima on Monday, we got a call from Nino, informing us that his house had been robbed that weekend. He had lost several computers and a significant amount of band equipment, most of which was Jaime's. Unfortunately *Pleno Verano* is also high season for robberies in Lima. The thieves correctly assume that many affluent houses will be left unoccupied or in the care of employees, since their owners are sure to be at the beach. Not easily dismayed, Jaime replaced the equipment; still the band had a lot of trouble getting together. There were too many mid-summer commitments.

That Wednesday we were invited to an elegant lunch in Tere's garden, complete with *mozos* serving in white jackets, black pants and bow ties. But the energy level was just as high in this setting as at the beach. As I rushed from one of the houses to catch up with a departing niece, I crashed headlong into a long tempered glass wall. BAM. Blood was everywhere; my blood. A quick trip to the Clínica Anglo-Americana emergency room in La Molina resulted in a call to a plastic surgeon in San Isidro, who battled almost an hour of traffic to put seven stitches in my lip. A day to recover and it was time to return to the beach.

That Friday night back at Conchitas, the lights went out at 11:30 p.m. We called the gate.

"*No se preocupe, Señor Jaime,*" Watson shouted into the phone. "They promise to have them back on by 7:00 tomorrow *evening.*"

"But, *why* did the lights go out this time?" Jaime groaned.

"Well, last night we heard a noise. We pointed our flashlight towards the road in time to get a quick view of several men stealing the electrical cables. They left behind a 30-foot bamboo pole with a new blade duct taped to the end, a number of tools, and the tracks of electrician's boots." These were no amateurs.

With no lights, we decided to head for Playa Asia. Outside the popular Wong grocery store were musicians playing *quenas,* Indian flutes from the mountains, and selling their CDs. Looking for a parking place, I saw eleven 18-wheelers and a 22-wheeler unloading soft drinks, ice, paper goods, and other essentials as fast as they could. The parking lot had turned into a staging area, reminiscent of supply distribution in times of crisis. Inside, Wong was as packed as a busy street market in Hong Kong. Everywhere in the shopping center, people were packed in by the thousands. Stores had begun their summer clearances, as they would all be empty and closed up for the winter in little more than a month. I could hear conversations in Spanish, English, French, and even German. Wading through the tightly-pressed bodies, I bumped into a man from Atlanta, easily identified by his rotund white body, colorful Hawaiian shirt, and big smile. He was surprised when I said "excuse me."

"How did you know I spoke English?" he asked, bewildered.

Just call it intuition.

Pleno Verano is a good time for fireworks, set off at the more populated beaches. When we got home, Conchitas was still without lights.

"Time to turn in for the night," I said. But even in the darkness, sleep was not to be. A beach somewhere to the north of us had begun their fireworks celebration. Surely in order to save money and prolong the excitement, their show began *just* after we went to bed, judiciously spacing the bangs about two minutes apart.

That night there were other late-night parties as well. We were awakened at 3:45 a.m. by heavy rock music coming from a neighbor's house. The music combined with my healing, yet throbbing, lip in an irregular syncopated beat.

Despite all the happenings, we were determined to enjoy ourselves. The electricity *did* come on the next night, just as the sun was setting. We'd just purchased a four-CD set of bossanovas, whose music flowed perfectly with the undulating waves and cool ocean breeze. Our guests that night enjoyed a dinner of chicken and *chorizo* (sausages) sizzling on

194

our large outdoor grill. For dessert Jaime peeled large ripe *higos* (figs) the size of plums, marinated them in red wine and honey, and covered the delightful mix with *queso de cabra* (goat cheese) from the nearby town of Chilca. As we enjoyed our late night dinner on the covered terrace, a full moon hung over the ocean, which glistened like diamonds rolling on a dark blue velvet cloth.

Like salmon making the lengthy journey upstream only to spawn and die, *Pleno Verano* took all year to reach its peak, then –– in a flash –– it was gone. How did we know that it had passed? That night, the rough surf with its red-flag warning of high tides and redistribution of sand was a sure sign. School would start back up the next week, emptying the beaches.

On Peru's central coast, summer is never long enough. The coastal mists settle in all too soon and last for as many months as the blazing sun does during the summer months in Texas. Each year we try to savor every drop of the Peruvian summer, like squeezing the juice out of a succulent orange. The Bible says "for everything there is a season," and it has never been more apparent to me than on a Peruvian beach. Happiness is a fleeting pleasure; one that should be enjoyed whenever it comes our way.

We have learned to enjoy the moment, even though the lights go out, the toilets overflow, there isn't enough food, someone is ill, my lip is stitched up, or even if there is a robbery.

Ana Teresa once told me, "If things are good, it's time to party. If they are about to get bad; better have a party. If they are already bad, all we can do is party."

I couldn't agree more.

A cozy fire warms the living room during the cold, clammy winter evenings.

18

A Season of Fire

On the night of the first anniversary of my mother's death, I found myself in a large asphalt parking lot, shivering in the heavy night mist, sadly reflecting on the irony of my life. If Mother were a Catholic and had lived and died in Lima, we would have held a *Misa del Año,* the traditional Peruvian mass to honor her wonderful life. But she was a fundamentalist who had lived in Texas, so the anniversary of her death went unnoticed. It was early spring in Lima. A time to prepare for the summer, but instead of a spirit of joyful preparation, I felt absolutely alone.

It was nearly 10 p.m. Jaime and I were standing with a smiling salesman, outside the Saga Falabella department store at the Jockey Plaza Mall. A large pallet laden with heavy cardboard boxes lay beside our car.

"*¿Entrariá?*" (Is it going it fit?), we asked the salesman.

"*Sí. ¡Por supuesto!*" (Yes. Of course!), replied the salesman, soles signs dancing in his eyes. We opened the trunk of our little, grey hatchback Peugeot to reveal – to our salesman's amazement – that it was absolutely brimming with *leña* (firewood), given to us when Tere's family removed an unfortunately-placed eucalyptus.

Leña is used by much of Peru's rural population for cooking. We instead used it in the living room fireplace to counteract the chilling effect of the walls of glass *mamparas*. The next morning we'd head south to restock the beach house. But first we had to get the furniture into the car. Jaime and the salesman began unboxing four patio chairs and a ten-foot diameter, cantilevered patio *sombrilla*. Since our two laptops and the digital cameras were inside, I maintained a watchful eye for any passersby who might grab our equipment and melt into the departing crowds. I occupied my mind trying to imagine how, in the morning, we might squeeze in an additional week's groceries and our suitcases.

The shuffling began in earnest: back seats folded to the front, *leña* towards the left (oh, there was so much of it), patio chair boxes to the right, the long *sombrilla* box thrust center and forward from the back window to the front windshield – umph! It fit. The salesman left with a smile and a shake of his head. Jaime and I squeezed into the front seats. The *sombrilla* box left just enough space for our heads, but no space to turn them to either side. We drove off into Lima's chaotic night traffic to Lichi's condo in San Isidro, where we left our car in her safe, but infernally small, basement parking space.

Each year we made our spring (October-November) trip to Peru not to rest, as many U.S. friends thought, but to escape the Texas ragweed season and to prepare for those precious summer weeks at the beach house. Spring temperatures in Lima vary between the mid-'50s and the low-'70s. With no heating in the houses and with humidity often over 90 percent, a little breeze could chill the bones.

Speaking of bones, during this Peru trip, Jorge organized a family side trip to Chiclayo over the last weekend that October. We made the 10-hour trip north at night via luxury bus, complete with sleeper seats and meals. What we did not see at night – but did see during the 12-hour return day trip – was an awesome landscape of beaches, dunes, deserts and mountains, broken abruptly by lush green fields of asparagus, potatoes, cotton, and sugar cane, wherever some enterprising company found a way to irrigate the desert. Navigating the sometimes steep curves around the mountains, the top floor of the double-decker Cruz del Sur bus swung back and forth, making us grateful for our nine privileged seats and private bath on the bottom floor.

We arrived at daybreak and were surprised to see how developed Chiclayo was. We were told it was the Lima of the north. The Spanish history of this area spoke of its exerted development efforts as far back as the 1600s, when it had hopes that a nearby city, Zaña, would become the capital of Peru. But floods of Biblical proportions, raids and years of destructive occupation by the notorious Frances Drake and other pirates eliminated all possibility of that. Now, Zaña is a dusty little town housing the ruins of several colonial churches. The sadness of those distant times is palpable to this day.

The lodge we rented had a modern *leña* kitchen, about the size of a living-dining room. This lodge was aptly named Los Horcónes, since its roof was supported by columns made of Y-shaped tree trunks. The word *horcón* in this case meaning a tree trunk shaped like a pitchfork. Water in the lodge was solar-heated – whenever management remembered to turn on the recirculation pumps. The thick walls were of adobe, covered with cement and painted bright blue and yellow. On the private terrace off our bedroom, I practiced my tai chi as the sun rose over the adjacent *huaca*, a dirt hill covering an ancient ruin.

That was truly the land of *leña,* with its vast, enchanted, desert forest of *algarrobo* trees and the resulting dead branches. The air had a certain haze, as if the swirling smoke from the burning *leña* mixed with the spirits of the dead, filling the air with mystery. We visited the archeological dig sites and museums of the brutal rulers Señor de Sipan, Señor de Sican, and Túcume. All three museums contained impressive collections of pre-Inca gold, pottery, and jewelry. We were most fortunate to come upon a friendly off-duty policeman who became our guide. His face, we all agreed, was an *exact* reproduction of the face on some local pre-Inca pottery. One museum had added a section on *curanderos* (Peruvian folk healers) to please the metaphysical tourists.

Curious about what metaphysical tourism entailed, I arranged a Halloween night jaunt with four of the other women in the group to a nearby *curandero*. Before we began, it sounded like it could be a lovely adventure, but it was *not* what I had expected.

For two hours, in the dark of a new moon, each of us heard the state of our luck. Fortunately, as I had organized the expedition, my luck was declared good. We participated in a removal of any stray foreign spirits and received *una buena floración* (a thorough floral ceremony).

During the first hour, the *curandero* drank from a clear, unlabeled bottle and began chanting. He called on his able assistant to guide each of us individually, in the dark, to the grassless yard. The assistant passed special mystical walking canes and small folk idols over our bodies, then shook off the invisible entities, apparently attached to the objects, stomping the ground and commanding them to depart. An hour later, the *floración* ceremony itself began. I had heard that this consisted of covering our bodies in some undefined way with flowers. *How sweet*, I thought. It was in fact, very sweet. We had sugar poured on our heads and were also asked to eat some of it. We drank sticky, heavily sugared water mixed with fragrant flower petals. This would have been enough to satisfy us, but much more was in store.

I learned a new Spanish word that trip, *escupir* (to spit), which would have been timely to know beforehand when asking about what the *curandero* did before the end of the *floración*. By the end of the ceremony, all five of us were covered not only in sugar but also with a moist film of strongly scented, spewed floral water. To top it off, the *curandero* told us to refrain from bathing until the next morning. That was perhaps a small feat for him, but I couldn't stop thinking, *Jaime is going to kill me!*

After hours of ritual chanting, the five of us gladly paid $15 apiece and left the *curandero's* house feeling gleeful. Were we cured of anything? Who knows? But after going through the ceremony together, we were light hearted, we felt the bond of sisterhood, and we certainly did smell like flowers.

Back in Lima, that spring left too much to describe. However, I can't help but mention some of the major events of the season.

To the Catholic, October is the season of devout women clothed in purple, in honor of El Señor de los Milagros, an elaborate Christ fresco painted on a prison wall by a slave named Pedro Dalcón. The faithful believe that this fresco is evidence of a miracle that occurred during a terrible earthquake in 1655, when an entire prison collapsed, except for this wall. This preserved wall contains a painting of a crucified Christ. Daily, tens of thousands of people pray to this image for healing – and it is believed that many healings actually do occur.

Once a year El Señor de los Milagros, weighing several tons, is taken from its resting place, at the main altar in the Santuario de Las Nazarenas in Lima, placed on a huge ceremonial platform, and borne through downtown Lima by crews of bent, penitent men. The wall and its platform are so heavy that the bearers must be relieved every block. The appeal of this miracle passes through all classes and nationalities, including a large percentage of Lima's educated women.

Instead of the Chiclayo smoke that smelled of *leña,* here fragrant incense filled the air. Watching the procession, I saw a man who both looked like and was dressed as Jesus, standing on an old balcony watching the parade. No one else seemed to even notice him. Instead, street vendors selling the sticky-sweet dense Turón de Doña Pepa with its tiny, multi-colored ball candy seemed to attract more attention.

We attended a *corrida de toros* (translated literally, the running of the bulls, but in English, a bullfight) at the famous, historically-pink Plaza de Acho, constructed in the 1700s, with its spontaneous half-time Marinera dancers and colorful embroidered Spanish shawls draped over the walls of the inner ring. Plaza de Acho is located across the Rimac River in a historic, yet dangerously rundown, part of the city. There, both vultures atop the walls and thieves outside the walls patiently awaited their rewards.

Opera season was in full swing, but that year there was no time for the opera house. Instead, we attended a presentation of *Don Juan Tenorio*, a mid-18th Century play by Spaniard José Zorrilla y Moral, held at night inside Lima's Presbítero Maestro, an elegant cemetery dating back to that timeframe and where many of Jaime's distinguished ancestors are interred.

During this change of seasons, death and life were intertwined. As I reflected back on the dead in the pre-Inca tombs around Chiclayo, I received an e-mail from my sister that our mother's grey granite gravestone had at last been installed. The marker contained not only our parents' names on the front, but ours on the back. The finality of this grounded my soul. I quickly focused on the many friends and family who were still living and doing very well. Among them was my dear father, who remained mentally alert and physically active. Mother's sister, Frances, turned 90, saying she couldn't find the time to stop to get old. In Lima we visited Tía Carmen, who was 92 and livelier, more enthusiastic, and more alert than many of us. All around us there was so much life, so much to enjoy. Thinking again of this season, the *leña* may have left only ashes, but we were on the way to the *sombrilla,* which brought with it a renewed life.

A second T'Anta restaurant had just opened with its highly popular, Nuevo-Peruvian cuisine. We were fortunate that it was just two short blocks down the street from Lichi's, where we were staying in Lima. As we headed for our temporary home after the play that night, we passed the perennial T'Anta traffic jam. Jaime jumped out of the car to grab our *tapas* dinner: medium-rare filet strips wrapped in eggplant, graced with fresh tomato sauce and topped with parmesan cheese, and mini-*tortillas* (thick Spanish potato pancakes). Back at Lichi's (she was away at the opera) we set an elegant table, popped the cork on a bottle of Rosso de Mistrosanti, lit two burnt-orange beeswax candles nestled in 19th Century silver candlesticks, turned on a CD of Antonio Carlos Jobim *bossanovas,* turned down the lights, and enjoyed being alive.

The next morning I sat at Lichi's little round dining table, on one of her antique Viennese bentwood and wicker Café Bistro chairs. Through a large picture window and past a windowsill supporting pots of flowering, succulent cactus, I contemplated the thick sage-green leaves adorning strong branches of the ancient, stories-tall olive trees in Parque El Olivar. On the round table were traces of burnt-orange candle wax. I smiled, remembering the night before. Suddenly words from my mother resound in my ears, "Enjoy your life now – don't wait."

Perhaps as a foreshadowing of what was to come, the song that wouldn't leave my head was an old Irving Berlin favorite, *Let's Face the Music and Dance.*

"There may be trouble ahead, so while there's music and moonlight and love and romance; let's face the music and dance."

Jaime had his own foreshadowing, playing Kansas' famous *Dust in the Wind* over and over again on his guitar.

"All we do... crumbles to the ground, though we refuse to see...

It slips away, and all your money won't another minute buy..."

What I could not know at that time was that the real *leña* was our Texas house. Within weeks of returning to Lake Jackson, on December 4th, our home full of memories and priceless collections would suffer a major fire. There were all our dreams – dust in the wind. The night of the fire we stayed at Dad's house. He presented us with two new toothbrushes, "I think you'll need these." We had literally nothing but the clothes on our backs.

It turned out the fire was only the beginning, as getting the city's approval to rebuild our house seemed impossible. Jaime struggled for weeks trying to redesign the house to meet the current regulations. The thick-skinned City Inspector was anything but helpful. Perhaps he did not understand the regulations himself. The worst part was that we had tickets to return to Lima in early January. As the days dragged painfully on, we began to despair of getting approval for the rebuild in time to return to the beach house for the Peruvian summer. Then, at 4:30 on the afternoon before we were to leave, Jaime chanced to call the City Inspector's office, inquiring about the approval.

"It's sitting right here on my desk," replied his secretary coldly.

So with that approval and total confidence in our builder, Manuel, we flew south, towards our *sombrilla*. Life had its priorities.

19

¡Paracas y Terremotos!

It was early morning and a chiffon yellow sun was rising over the camel brown hills. Steel grey clouds still hung heavy over the ocean that laid itself out at my feet in a broad panorama. My computer, located in the downstairs bedroom, and most other appliances were working, thanks to Jaime's quick mind and skillful hands. I've often reflected on how this "heaven" would be my own personally-tailored "hell," if not for his presence. Jaime always found a way to make everything work again.

The past few days had featured a series of significant weather *inconveniences*. Who could assess a more onerous name when it never really rained, froze, or stormed on the desert coast of Peru? Our U.S. friends couldn't believe it, but we didn't have tornadoes or hurricanes. There was a tremor now and then, as the tectonic plates offshore rubbed together, but all in all, it was a peaceful place.

The recent weather inconvenience – *la paraca* – had arrived at Conchitas three days before. Though related, this unusual weather should not be confused with the Peruvian coastal city of the same name. That Paracas was the site of San Martin's vision of flamingos that created the red and white Peruvian flag, and today is the launching point of tourist boats heading for the Ballestas Islands. Though uninhabited by humans, this group of small islands is the natural refuge for seals, Peruvian Penguins, Red-Footed Cormorants, and Inca Terns. No, this story was about the infamous *paraca* – the coastal sandstorms for which that city was named.

We had been in Lima for a two-night stay at Lichi's condo. That first day, Jaime came down with *la gripe*, a bad case of the flu that seemed to be encircling the globe in the wake of the recent tsunami that so terribly hit the South Pacific area.

Jaime's case was contracted in Texas, but it didn't seem to matter where one was, there were cases showing up everywhere. The young seemed to fare pretty well with a day of fever. The old were faring very badly though, sometimes dying. Fortunately, Jaime was in the middle age group and the fever lasted *only* seven days. Unfortunately, it was followed by two days of severe leg cramps, thanks to a "rarely encountered" counter-indication of the antibiotic, Cipro®. During that time he grew despondent, as our vacation slipped away.

Nine days after our arrival in the country, Doris arrived in time for breakfast. The three of us emerged from Lichi's condo, antsy to get moving and headed down south on the *Panamericana* to our favorite kilometer. Driving southward from Lima for over an hour, we passed the resort communities at Playa Asia and were heading past the indigenous village of Rosario and towards Pasamayito, that dynamited break in the table mountain allowing the *Panamericana* to pass through. At that moment, our car was struck from the right by an invisible force that felt as if we'd been hit by a truck.

"What was *that*?" I exclaimed.

A thick layer of sand began covering the road ahead of us. Judging from the direction of the wind and the accumulating sand, we realized it had to be a strong air current blowing straight off the ocean. Our little Peugeot pulled more roughly towards the driver's side. Jaime gripped the steering wheel as hard as he could. I was scared. My heart beat so hard, I thought it was going to burst.

"This feels like something out of Raiders of the Lost Ark," I shouted over the dinning noise of the sandstorm. "What do you think it is?"

"*¡PARACA!*" Jaime and Doris screamed, in unison.

Visibility instantly dropped to ten feet. We slid into the left lane, hoping to avoid the drifts. The sand kept coming, forcing us to slow our pace. Focusing on a truck in front of us, we were able to navigate the pass, then move past the hill labeled Zona de Neblina, the foggy area, and begin the descent towards Conchitas.

When we reached the Conchitas front gate, Watson, the chief guard, ran out holding his hat on his head.

"*Señor* Jaime," he began in his rough, semi-screaming voice, "looks like we've got a *paraca*. No one has any idea how long it will last. The wind is blowing at about 80 miles per hour right now."

Indeed.

The sky was mustard yellow, filled with sand. The usual breathtaking view down to the horseshoe beach totally obscured. I looked at my watch. It was 3:10 p.m. At a snail's pace, we descended the winding road that led to our house, carefully avoiding the steep drop to the beach at the T-intersection. Finally reaching the house, we quickly exited, grabbed some of our things, closed up the car, and unlocked the door of the outside wall. The wind was swirling its blinding sand through the air. Our black suitcases were rapidly turning a dusty, sandy yellow. We quickly unlocked the inner doors and ran inside ensuring all the windows and glass *mampara* sliding walls were closed. The three of us worked as fast as possible, stuffing moist towels under the doors and the window sills. Then, because our house was built in modules with hallways open to the sky, we closed ourselves off in the living/dining room and kitchen, in sweltering stagnation, and watched our lovely bougainvilleas, lantanas, and geraniums be torn to shreds. It took hours for the *paraca* to tire itself out. During that time we could see nothing outside but sand blowing horizontally in the wind. Even the view to the beach, some 100 feet below, was completely obscured. As we sat impotently, watching the storm rage, we read every page of days-old newspapers, and advertisements we would normally have thrown away, reorganized the CD collection, and talked out every conceivable subject.

"Face it," I said, "we're trapped. I hate to see the damage to our new paint job when this is finally over."

"Let's hope the paint is all that is damaged," worried Jaime, fearing he'd have even more repairs on his hands. As the dim daylight began to fade, we watched tall sand drifts accumulate against the *mamparas,* eventually creeping into the house.

Needless to say, a *paraca* was the bane of anyone who owned a white house. Yet most Peruvian beach communities, including ours, were filled with white houses. Our beach house had been painted only a month ago and had been a brilliant white.

Sometime after sunset, the howling wind began to die down. Since we had lost power, Doris prepared and served us a simple *caldo de gallina* by candlelight. Early bedtime was the only logical option since there was nothing else we could do.

We awoke to a cloudy morning and found the desert quite literally on our doorstep; our pristine white paint wore a fresh coat of yellow sandblast. Since our house comprised many separate areas, with the staircase and most of the doors on the outside, the degree of sand damage was depressing. Our newly-refinished antique colonial wooden doors were caked with sand; the infinity pool harbored a mini-beach on its bottom. Even our precious flowers, the recipient of so much expensive water, were crusted with sand, and some of the branches were broken, dried and nearly dead.

The cleanup began after breakfast. We called in Violeta, the reinforcement maid. To avoid doing double work, it seemed to me that sand removal should begin with the rooftops and work downward. Doris had a better idea. She directed all four of us in the cleanup operation, which progressed by area most frequently used: first the living/dining room/kitchen, next the terrace, afterward our bedroom overhead, and lastly the maid's bedroom. Even with the four of us working as hard as we could, the cleanup continued through that day and the next. All around us teams of people worked on our neighbors' houses in a similar manner. At the end of day two, our rooms were fairly clean, but still the only habitable sleeping quarters were our bedroom and the maid's quarters. We were fortunate that we didn't have guests! Only one of the five roof areas was clean and the ocean side of the house still harbored hills of sand. Thank goodness it never rained there. Well, *almost* never.

"Listen, I hear water running," I said at breakfast. "Is a pipe broken?"

"Marie, that's rain," said Jaime. "Can't you hear the drops?"

"Ah, drops. I've never actually heard *raindrops* at this beach. Maybe this will be enough to wash the house clean."

But the "rain" was not enough to wash off the remaining sand, only to make it stick. Once the water began drying, the surrounding hills took on a ghostly appearance as the moisture drew the nitrates, or *salitre,* to the surface, forming large, intermittent layers of crusty white on the dunes, foothills, and even some of the concrete sidewalks made using local sand. Our second floor bedroom patio filled with water, as did the downstairs terrace. Doris and Violeta mopped and mopped. Mopping and sand removal continued through day three. The sun did not break through the clouds all day. At the end of the day, exhausted, we knew we had done all we could for the time being. We decided to relax and watch some TV. We sat down, pressed the "On" button, and witnessed a small explosion. *Oh dear!*

The morning of day four, I arose just before dawn and made myself a cup of frothy cappuccino. In the main room, I put on Sarah Brightman's *Classics* album and walked to the window, looking down on the beach. I gazed through the recently-cleaned glass *mamparas* into a cloudless, crystalline blue sky. A gentle, dry breeze blew in off the ocean. As Sarah began singing *Ave María,* a chiffon yellow sun rose over the Andean foothills to my right, illuminating the cliffs surrounding our beach. The freshly cleaned white houses once again reflected the radiant morning light, creating a picture-postcard-perfect contrast against the deep sapphire ocean below. Franklin Gulls, just arrived from the snowy North American plains, glided smoothly at eye level past our hillside perch, their black wings and snow-white breasts glowing in the morning sun. Was I the only human witnessing this panorama? Tears of gratitude rolled down my cheeks.

"Thank you, God, for letting me be a part of all of this!"

Looking beyond what was left of our brick-red bougainvillea hedge and down to the beach, the recently-scrubbed royal blue *sombrillas* were shining in the sunrise, sporting neatly aligned rows of shadows to their left. Workers were already raking the beach to create the perfect finish for us to enjoy later in the day. As Sarah began singing *Lascia Chi'o Pianga* and then *O Mio Bambino Caro,* a flock of Grey Pelicans entered the scene from the north, floating in a perfect "V" formation just above the ocean's surface on their flight to the south. The entire beach took on a holy air, as if sanctified by the ordeals of the days before. There was the tremendous spiritual feeling of cleanliness on that last morning; the feeling of being the only person witnessing nature show off its finest, just for me. It was literally the "quiet after the storm."

All I could think was how blessed we were. What did I ever do to deserve living here? How could I ever repay this gift? All I knew to do was to record the memory in my meager words.

Bless this place. Praise the Giver. Breathe in the moment. Try, try to hold on to the memory.

But that would not be the only weather event we survived. Years later, on a hot August night in Texas, Jaime and I were watching TV when a news bulletin broke in. "Severe earthquake hits the central Peruvian coast north of the city of Pisco," was the message.

"*How* severe?" I shouted at the TV. "Our beach house is north of Pisco!"

Desperate calls to the family in Lima assured us that they were all fine, with the exception of Jorge, who had just returned to his condo on the 14th floor, located on a cliff facing the ocean. His lights went out immediately and it was dark outside. Then a large water line broke on the roof, flooding his condo. All the while the building was being thrashed around like a toy baseball bat. He survived, but was quite shaken up.

We called Jaime's band friend Nino, a PhD structural engineer who lived in the La Molina district to the east. "My house is completely structurally sound, but for several *minutes* it moved back and forth over *a yard* in either direction," he said.

Lima was several hundred miles to the north of the epicenter. What of the beach house? We tried calling the beach gate, but the lines were down. The next day we were able to get through.

"Watson, how are you? How are our houses?" we asked anxiously.

"Ah, *Señor* Jaime," he said with a strained voice. "It was terrible. The ground turned to *jello* for three full minutes. Then there were the aftershocks. We thought they would never stop. There was nowhere to go. Roque has been in your house. There are several broken *mamparas*. He took the other ones down. We are all scared of what will happen now."

"You mean our house is open to the *air*?" we exclaimed.

"*Sí*, but it is better off than your next door neighbor's house. Their house broke apart and slid part-way down the hill. The toilets are still attached to their pipes, but are standing a foot in the air. Part of their roof is caved in. The only good news is that it wasn't summer, so none of you were here. Don't worry about us. We'll be OK ... I think."

Three days later we flew into Lima and headed immediately to our beach. Lima appeared largely untouched, but not the *Panamericana*. The further south we got and the closer to the epicenter, the more light poles were broken and the more houses collapsed. In some areas, the intercontinental highway itself was destroyed. We stopped at our beach, frantic to see the destruction, and scared to go any further. Our house had survived with only "minor" damage, which took over five months to repair. We had no insurance in Peru. It had been just over a year since our house in Texas had suffered a major fire, where fortunately we *did* have insurance. The poor people to the south in Pisco and surrounding areas had none. We still don't know when or if some of those areas will be rebuilt.

As I look back on these times, it is clear how the best of plans can be ruined by things totally out of our control. The things we take for granted sometimes fail, bringing us into a whole new realm of awareness.

After the Texas house fire and the Peru earthquake, I better understand the value of our lives versus our property, the value of having a talented and dedicated husband, the closeness we felt to our employees, without whom cleaning up after the storm and the house reconstruction would have been virtually impossible. No matter what happens, at the end of each day, having a loving family and a good support system is all that really matters.

At this particular wedding, the Olympic-size swimming pool had been converted into a fountain. Around the sides were life-size carved marble statues. In the back of the park were expanses of semi-sheer white "toldos," as the Peruvian architectural tents are called. We walked over Persian rugs towards the elegantly dressed crowd.

20

Weddings

Weddings, called *matrimonios* or *bodas* in Spanish, are the most significant of a lifetime packed full of social occasions. This is nothing new, as everywhere in the world weddings are the most elaborate and enduring of all events. It goes without saying that there is no more exciting event than a good wedding, and Peruvians always make the most of any situation. Peruvian weddings are not to be missed. On a few occasions, we have flown from Texas to Lima for a *weekend* to attend a special family wedding. Peruvian weddings are so relatively affordable and can be so fabulous that some couples choose Peru for their destination wedding.

It is easy to notice some of the external differences between weddings in the U.S. and in Peru. For one, there is no rehearsal dinner in Peru, the important event which in the U.S. falls to the groom's family. In Peru the groom's family pays for everything associated with the church, including flowers, priest, musicians, and decorations. The bride's family traditionally pays for everything related to the party afterward, which can be quite elaborate. Invitations to weddings are discreet white cards with engraved black lettering and are hand delivered in a single envelope. I don't know whether this delivery method is due to the importance of the invitation or the reliability of the Peruvian postal system. Perhaps it is a little of both. As weddings are often enormous, key family members are each given a batch of invitations to deliver.

In Peru, silver is the most notable wedding gift. The number of silver platters the couple receives is an indication of the wealth and influence of the family and their friends. Today, china, crystal, appliances, and other practical articles are increasingly given as well. Traditionally, the gifts are displayed on shelves set up in the home of the bride, along with the calling card of each of the givers. As in the U.S., honeymoons in Peru are the responsibility of the groom. In the Peruvian newlyweds' home, the groom is traditionally responsible for acquiring the house itself, furniture, large appliances, and other "hard" objects; the bride provides kitchenware, towels, sheets, draperies, and other "soft" items. An old Peruvian custom was the groom giving *arras,* or money, to the bride to prove he would be able to provide for them. Today this custom is rarely followed, since many brides already have their own careers.

Looking more deeply, in Peru a proper bride and groom do not marry young. They are expected to know each other quite well, and many relationships go back to the early- to mid-teenage years. Their families' inter-relationships can go back for generations, some of them even having distant relatives in common. Although the custom of families knowing each other and being interrelated persists in some affluent parts of the northeast U.S., much of the rest of the population doesn't have that luxury, because the country is so large and people are so mobile.

In Peru, the wedding ceremony consists of two distinct ceremonies: the legal and the religious. Thus the phrase in a popular Peruvian song, *"Ante Díos y el Registro Civil,"* in front of God and the Civil Registry. Sometimes these ceremonies are held on separate days, weeks, or even months. After the religious ceremony, there is a reception in the cloisters of the church. At this event, guests pass through the traditional greeting line and champagne is served from tall flutes. The reception should never be confused with the wedding *party,* which is held at another location and requires a separate invitation.

There are several stages of the wedding party, all liberally sprinkled with the best alcohol the family can afford. The party begins with hors d'oeuvres served by *mozos* in white jackets, followed by the feast itself, often a large buffet. This is sometimes intermingled with and always followed by dancing. Lastly, and for many most importantly, is the confection table, filled with beautiful hand-made sweets presented in the most creative ways. Cutting the cake, the highlight of most U.S. wedding parties, is somewhat insignificant in Peru, occurring between midnight and daybreak, and sometimes not at all. Dancing until the guests collapse is a given. Often, a sunrise breakfast is served, before the final guests depart.

The most beautiful wedding I have yet attended was of a female relative, an architect, who married her fiancée, a lawyer. The families knew each other and the couple were well matched.

We landed in Lima on a Friday night in the fall, ready to celebrate. I believe it was mid-May.

The wedding ceremony was held on a Saturday evening in a large stone church in San Isidro. The reigning Cardinal officiated, as the church's main organ played and the National Choir sang their repertoire. The elegant golden Baroque altar at the Cardinal's back rose forty feet high and boasted beautiful statues of the Virgin Mary and Child and the saints.

The bride, adorned in an understated white strapless floor-length gown, wore her great-grandmother's fragile European lace veil that flowed down past her gown and trailed on Persian carpets. In her hands was a simple batch of large red rosebuds, tied together with a white satin ribbon. Waiting at the altar were her mother and *suegra*, mother-in-law, on the left side. On the right was the groom and the father of the bride, the head of a prominent law firm and arguably one of the most handsome and imposing men in Lima. Behind the bride were several lovely little flower girls, dressed in white. As was the custom in Peru, there was no ring bearer, and no bridesmaids or groomsmen. The wedding altar was not the place for friends; this was a solemn family religious ceremony.

During the ceremony a few intimate friends walked up to the podium to read from the Bible. The words of the wedding ceremony are etched in the heart of all, regardless of what language they are said, and always end in, "What God has joined together let no man tear asunder." A kiss, a walk down the aisle, and their new life together had begun. Following the religious ceremony, there was the signing of the civil marriage paperwork. Afterward we were guided to the church cloisters for a brief champagne reception. Then we all went home to regroup.

About 9:30 p.m., we arrived at a private park in a quiet residential neighborhood where the wedding *party* was to be held. Several uniformed guards were directing on-street parking. The bride had chosen this location because it was there that she had for many years played in safety, away from the dangers that led parents to protect their children during the fearful years before Alberto Fujimori's presidency captured the terrorists and stabilized the country.

Walking up to what seemed like nothing more than a white wall over which spilled pink bougainvilleas, we were greeted cordially by several tall, untanned, immaculately-suited and handsome bodyguards standing in front of a three-foot wide, polished, locked wooden door with a wrought-iron handle and peephole. One of them carefully checked our

IDs and our personalized invitations, smiling as he bowed genteelly and opened the door.

Once inside, we followed a rocky pathway that led through a small but fragrant rose garden, then walked towards the lights, through the lobby of the private clubhouse with its polished sandstone floor, and into a large, perfectly manicured garden, full of tall eucalyptus trees. In the distance we could see huge, white *toldos*, filled with elegantly-attired guests.

"Looks like we are in for *some* wedding party," I swooned.

We walked over Persian rugs and past more than a half dozen life-size marble statues that graced the sides of the lighted Olympic-length swimming pool, illuminated that evening by a 20-foot-high central fountain. Beyond the end of the pool we were greeted by the first of many *mozos* in short white jackets, black pants, and black bow ties. He came offering tall goblets of excellent French champagne, a bottle of which he had removed from an enormous bowl-shaped ice sculpture, complete with an ice pedestal base. Frozen into the sides of the ice punch bowl were large, red rosebuds.

Entering the *toldos* to the left, we were greeted by dozens of family members and friends. More white-jacketed *mozos* offered over a dozen types of hors d'oeuvres and canapés, artfully arranged on silver platters. After an hour or so of champagne, canapés and mingling, the *mozos* escorted us to the larger adjoining *toldo* complex to the right. My eyes struggled to adjust to the scale of the space. Large round tables, seating ten people, each were covered most elegantly with layers of flowing white tablecloths and topped by silver service plates, layers of china, an array of silver flatware, and several sizes of matching crystal stemware. In the middle of each of what must have been over two hundred tables was a large arrangement of enormous red Ecuadorian rosebuds. I remember thinking that they must have chartered a cargo plane for the roses alone. On every table was a one-liter bottle of Johnny Walker Black Label. We found our table by looking through the calligraphed place cards.

Just as we were getting seated and were being served our choice of Merlot or Chardonnay, there was a squeal from several of the bride's friends, followed by a mad dash, as tuxes and formals rustled towards the long sushi bar that had just been opened. In those days, sushi was still a distant novelty in Texas, so I must admit to having forgone this delicacy. But that luxury was not lost on the couple and their friends, who devoured every last bite in moments.

I glanced toward the dance floor, located in the middle of the tables. It was illuminated by a huge suspended metal framework supporting what at first appeared to be dozens of votive candles, but which turned out to be full-sized hurricane lamps.

My attention was drawn back to the people at our table, who were discussing the long mirror-image buffet tables, located at the edges of either side of the *toldos*, and staffed by *mozos*. There was food to satisfy the palette of the most discriminating gourmet, from seafood to prime rib, each presented as one might arrange a large batch of flowers in a five-star hotel lobby. A number of the dishes were presented with their own ice sculptures. My favorite was a three-foot high sculptured ice "peacock" whose tail was made totally from boiled, shelled shrimp. At the end of the main buffet tables were shorter tables filled with unusual breads and cheeses.

As we finished the buffet, the Blue Danube began to play, and the bride joined her father on the dance floor. When the second dance began, the groom interrupted and the happy couple danced together. In the dances that followed, the bride and groom and their parents were joined by other immediate family members, and afterward friends and more distant relatives. The source of all this music was well out of sight, behind a series of screened panels situated near an outside wall.

It wasn't until the dancing began in earnest that my attention turned to the evening gowns. Every one was floor length, many sequined. Mature women wore silk formals in blues, greens, silver and black, their pearls, diamonds, emerald necklaces, earrings, and rings glittering. The young women wore little jewelry and their gowns were tastefully made, exposing just enough of the body to make viewing interesting. This was the first time I saw formals made from shiny stretch material, which clung to the young women's perfectly-proportioned and well-toned bodies, each displaying a golden tan. Some of the formals had open, laced backs, revealing lovely expanses of skin. The young women wore their blonde or brown hair straight and either shoulder- or waist-length. They moved back and forth to the increasingly lively beat of *merengues,* their hair shaking and shining in the candlelight like the manes of the thoroughbreds they were.

At one point the music was toned down and photos began. I remember the new couple standing there with huge smiles: handsome, slim, and erect with the dignity of people who were confident in themselves. They were both born into their station in life and had worked hard to establish careers to maintain their lifestyles.

Around midnight the former sushi table was reincarnated into an espresso bar, complete with a variety of flavored biscotti. On the distant opposite side of the *toldo* was a forty-foot long dessert table, adorned with a number of cupid ice sculptures and filled with ambrosial confections that challenged the imagination, every one of them handmade for this wedding. There were three-foot high cones filled with swirling white, cream-colored, milk- and dark-chocolate bon-bons. On large silver platters of varying heights there were artful arrangements of *lúcuma* creams, petits fours, and the smallest dark chocolate truffle-filled boxes wrapped with white chocolate ties. To balance that off, white chocolate boxes stood alongside, wrapped with dark chocolate ties. Although I wasn't alone in gorging on the heavenly delights, I remember personally consuming, among other things, a number of those little chocolate boxes and at least five small white chocolate baskets filled with *lúcuma* cream. Yum!

We danced to Latin rhythms until I couldn't stand up any more. At 3:00 a.m. I inquired, "When are they going to cut the cake? I always heard that it is *bad luck* for people to leave a wedding before the cake is served."

The word was quickly passed about potential bad luck, and the enormous confection, architecturally designed by the bride, "iced" with long vertical slivers of white chocolate, and covered with red rose petals, was finally served.

Sometime before sunrise, we headed toward the door. We were utterly exhausted, but that was to be expected. We said goodbye to the newlyweds and their parents, and to the rest of our extended family. As we left, I complimented the mother-of-the-bride, resplendent in her flowing royal blue sequined gown, every blonde hair still in place, on having pulled off the most beautiful wedding I had ever seen.

"How did you *do* this?" I asked. "It was all so, so *fabulous!*"

"*Con tiempo, paciencia y mucho, mucho amor,*" she replied, smiling and giving me a big hug and a good night kiss. With time, patience and a whole lot of love.

As we passed the guards, one gave me his business card. It showed their company was out of Salt Lake City, with an office in Lima.

"If you need anything, *any* thing," he said in unaccented English looking me in the eye, "all you have to do is call and it will be taken care of."

The honor of being invited inside the walls to attend significant social occasions, especially weddings, and of being related to the resulting closely-knit newly expanded families, has given me wonderful insights into Peruvian lifestyles. This is not a culture where children go off to college, marry someone the parents do not know, and then move away forever. To this day, it is the norm for offspring of all social classes to live in the parents' house until they marry. When the time is right, which is usually somewhere in the mid- to late-20s, parents of at least a certain strata generally *know* and *approve* of the potential mate, as well as the family that their child is marrying into. Since they have often known the family for some time, they are better able to predict the behavior of the new son- or daughter-in-law and the success of the marriage.

Language tells us so much about a culture. In the U.S. we women lose our maiden names when we marry, or at best carry them as middle names. In Latin countries, women *always* keep their maiden names, adding a *de* after that and before their husband's last name. Children carry two last names, first their father's, followed by their mother's. The phone book is organized so the members of one family are naturally grouped together by both last names. For example, my name in Spanish is really quite simple: Marie Elena McNair Fernandez Santa Eulalia de Alvarez Calderón. Lamentably, my maternal grandparents, while living in New York City, were driven to reissue all their children's birth certificates, dropping two of their three last names in the process, because clerks in the birth registrar's office wrote the names incorrectly on *all four* of their children's birth certificates. Today the males in the family carry only the generic and untraceable last name of Fernandez.

Through the years, I have seen how very different my marriage to Jaime must have been viewed by his family, and am even more grateful that they accepted me into their lives. It is now clear that there is no standard formula for a marriage or a life to evolve.

As a teen my mother had warned me against marrying a Latin man, yet by doing just that, my life became what I had dreamed it would be. In a sense, my destiny has been realized the reverse of what I had planned. Indeed, the summer of my life came not in July, but in February.

Epilogue

When I am in the U.S. I remember Conchitas beach conceptually – the hills reaching down to the sea, the horseshoe beach, our small community of 30 houses. In my mind, I walk through our house, room by room. But what I so desperately want to capture is the *feeling* of this moment.

The sun is gently rising to my right, illuminating the hills with a golden glow. The white sides of the blocky modern beach houses are glowing pure in the new light. Freshly-painted white Adirondack chairs are neatly clustered beneath our *sombrillas*, their tops shining bright royal blue – the shadows they cast to the left are elongated in the early light.

A long expanse of immaculate suede-colored sand is a stopping-off ground for hundreds of birds, who have come from as far away as Chile and North America, in their own groupings of white, grey, and black. Below our hill and to the left of the beach are gently undulating waves. As they reach the shore, their bright white foam sparkles in the morning light. Beyond that is the vast ocean – always the ocean – today almost as docile as a boundless lake. There is a breeze that blows across my body from the hills to the sea, like the finest silk chiffon being pulled by Mother Nature herself.

Perhaps stirred by the breeze, the birds rise in unison, looking for breakfast in the cool sea. Waves crash against rocks that thousands of years ago may have been hills – just like the one our house sits on today. Two fishermen, their dark-brown skin shining bright in the morning sun, navigate the steep hill to my left, laying their lines for the morning catch. The only sounds are the sea and the birds. A solitary figure practices yoga on the shore below. I look back onto the patio to see the awakening of the rows of *dormilonas*, the traffic yellow sleeping flowers, planted in front of the bougainvilleas, their blooms glowing brick-red in the morning light.

Again, I am at one with the universe. It is a sacred moment; a time of ecstasy.

During the years of writing this memoir, friends have assured me that I've changed a lot – morphing from a *gringa* to a *criolla*, the term many Peruvians use to identify someone who is part of their culture. Although I am only slightly more proficient in Spanish, I am no longer afraid to join a conversation. Today, instead of holding back when the salsa music starts, I'm one of the first on the floor. "Ah Marie, you are *bien* Latina," one of my tai chi companions said at a recent charity luncheon.

People often ask how we fill our time, going back and forth so often. In both Peru and in the U.S. our lives are full. It is just that in Peru, they are full of different things: especially social commitments and time with family and friends – building relationships.

What will the future hold? None of us can ever know. But here on my beach house patio, I've learned to focus on the present.

What I know for sure is that God has given me this perfect time in my life – this perfect morning. I will be silent and appreciate it. It is more than I ever thought possible. It is more than enough.

Beach House Meditation Messages

One summer's day, some years ago, I sat for hours on the patio off our second-floor master bedroom, meditating while focusing on the open ocean. I emptied my mind and sat very still. I received these seven messages, which I wrote on a yellow post-it note and have carried with me ever since. When all else is stripped away, these messages help me regroup and stabilize in this constantly changing world.

- Judge not, that you be not judged
- Show the way
- Find beauty in all things
- Serve as you have been served
- Speak kind words
- Imagine the best in everyone
- Believe and act and it will come to pass

May your life be blessed. May you think good thoughts, live a full life, and be able to meet, respect, and perhaps love people from all over the world. And may all your dreams, no matter how improbable, eventually come true.

One summer's day while meditating on this patio, the above messages came to me.

My parents, Howard and Dot, c. 1946, in their own
paradise on the island of Oahu, Hawaii.

Acknowledgements

I could not have had the experiences to fill this book if it were not for my dear husband, Jaime, with whom I lived this memoir.

To his family and friends who have opened their homes and their hearts, inviting me to pass through the portals into their private world behind the walls, I love you dearly and hope that I have represented you fairly.

To my parents, who raised me with sincere respect for people from other cultures, provided me with a firm foundation in the Christian faith, and who set an example of generosity, self-control, and devotion that would be impossible to match.

To Peruvian artist Rubén Aponte, whose art continues to speak to my spirit, regardless of life's changing circumstances. The perfection of his oil paintings reaches the sublime.

To our Peruvian employees, Doris, Roque, Veronica and her husband Santos, who continue to make possible our comfortable and gracious lifestyle in Lima and at the beach.

To Nan Hall Linke, my personal advisor, who encouraged me to bring this manuscript to the public at this time.

To Max Regan, who advised me on the organization and content of this book.

To John Arvin and Tom Morris, the naturalists who gave me names of the birds we live with on the Peruvian Coast.

To Jorge Alvarez-Calderon, who clarified my cultural interpretations, memories of the family, and improved my Spanish.

To Paige Marie Reeves, who is familiar with many of the places and people in this book and who polished my sentences until they flowed smoothly. To Judy Armstrong, who can find a typo in a haystack.

To peer reviewers Sylvia Jenson, Ana Teresa Velarde, Ana Maria Villanueva, Sharon Moore, and Kay Sommerlatte, who gave me key insights into the way of both Peruvian and U.S. readers would perceive this book.

And lastly, to Peru: an exquisite country that can never be thought of as "ordinary."

About the Author

Born on the island of Oahu to a vivacious Latin theatrical dress designer from New York City and a quiet, studious chemical engineer from Hearne, Texas, Marie McNair Alvarez-Calderón grew up south of Houston.

She spent 30 years working for a Fortune 500 petrochemical company. Supporting technical documentation, she traveled to scores of plant sites spanning five continents, learning to respect and admire people of many cultures.

In 1987, Marie married Peruvian-born Jaime Alvarez-Calderón, engineer and father of three children. The two have traveled extensively, returning to Peru over 65 times. They are now retired and divide their time between their families and houses in the U.S. and Peru.

Check out Marie's website: www.marieac.com

www.ingramcontent.com/pod-product-compliance
Lightning Source LLC
Chambersburg PA
CBHW022128050726
47590CB00002B/453